DISTANCE 01

concerns *beginnings.*

Wherein:

Benjamin Jackson discusses the problems with new conventions in game design.

Jon Whipple writes about how to instititionalize research among teams in an agency.

Vitorio Miliano analyzes how to improve the activities of local professional communities.

❃

DISTANCE's essays don't exist in a vacuum. We encourage you to excerpt and discuss these essays with others. You have free reign to quote as much as you need to get your point across. Good writing begins conversations, and we're listening.

Visit *Distance*'s website at http://distance.cc to read and remark on others' responses. If you received this copy as a gift, you're also owed a **digital bundle** of PDF, ePub, and Kindle versions to highlight and excerpt at your leisure. We don't believe in your paying twice for the same thing. Contact us at we@distance.cc and we'll make it right.

About DISTANCE

Distance is a full-assed attempt at publishing serious, long-form writing about design. It contains three long articles by really talented practitioners. We then put those articles into a nice pocketbook, we print two thousand copies of it, and then those copies are sold through the internet, straight from us to you. We try to avoid middlemen, so we edit, design, pack, and ship the whole print run. And finally, when we run out of each issue, we run out for good, and you'll have to buy the digital bundle instead.

We do what we can to make each issue great, we charge readers a fair price, we pay writers a fair price, and we try not to be a jerk to anybody. Hopefully you like all of this. We think it makes sense; we think it's the right thing to do.

It's entirely possible that somebody else loaned or gave this to you. That means they think you're an exceptional person. You should reward them, perhaps with beer or a good meal. But it also means that you probably don't know what we're all about, and this page is here to help. You know what else is here to help? Our website, which is at http://distance.cc. You can learn more about us there if you'd like.

We hope you're having a good day.

Note on citations

Distance exists in quite a few forms: book, PDF, ePub, and Kindle. We know that people read all sorts of ways, and we want the text to fit your reading habits, not the other way around. 1

Most citation methods refer to a work's page number, but only two of *Distance*'s forms have discrete pages. Consistent, understandable citation by page number is impossible, so wayfinding must exist within the actual text. 2

In an attempt to solve this problem, *Distance* doesn't have page numbers. Instead, each essay's paragraph has a little number to the right, as seen here. *These numbers will always be consistent among each format of an issue of* Distance. 3

This is similar to the convention of "purple numbers" in blogging,[1] and it will remove any ambiguity about what's being referenced. As a rule of thumb, where a page number would go, use the **paragraph number** instead. 4

For example, MLA citation should look like Whipple, Jon. "What Designers Know." *Distance* 01: 14-17 for the 14th through 17th paragraphs of Jon Whipple's essay in this issue. 5

1. See also CIM Community, "Purple Numbers", http://dsn.tc/01x-01 and Simon Willison, "PLinks", http://dsn.tc/01x-02.

Authors' thanks

Benjamin Jackson would like to thank his editor, Nick Disabato, for his undying patience and cordial manner; his roommates, Adam Wallace and Judson Stephenson, for indulging his constant chatter about stupid Facebook games for three months straight; Benjamin Brooks and Craig Grannell, both of whose writing inspired the initial essay which led to the piece; Mike Krahulik and Jerry Holkins, whose discussion of Skinner's work on *Penny Arcade* TV helped shape the core argument considerably; Max Temkin for providing tons of links and early feedback on the initial ideas in the piece; and all of the wonderful, attractive, young-for-their-age backers who helped make this first issue possible.

Jon Whipple: I would like to thank Nick Disabato for the opportunity to learn more about what I think and to share it with you.

Vitorio Miliano: This essay would have been a handful of anecdotes with a spoonful of conjecture without the primary research graciously afforded by IxDA Austin and Austin UPA.

Tori Breitling and Julie Lowe granted me access to their groups' historical data and, with Kyra Edeker and Amy Jones, caught me up on years of local color.

Craig Tomlin provided recent UPA group data, and Dr. Llewyn Paine offered substantial insight, statistical analysis and consulting on the new survey.

Alex Jones (Refresh Austin) and Dr. Clay Spinuzzi (University of Texas) provided additional feedback and support on an early draft.

Chris Avore recommended Wenger's *Communities of Practice*, and Joel Bush recommended Block's *Community: The Structure of Belonging*. Scott Dudley, Andrew Risch, Erik Smartt, Maria Joseph, and Justin Skolnick retrospectively provided additional insight.

Editor's thanks

by **Nick Disabato**
nickd@nickd.org, @nickd

After a lot of work and patience (which is a kind of work), at last: the first issue of *Distance*.

We have so many great places to write about design, but I believe that *Distance* is a different thing: theory and high-level ideas geared towards practitioners. Towards that end I'm grateful for the backers who took us on faith to publish this, sight unseen.

To the authors of this issue: *Distance* couldn't have been a thing without you, and I'm eternally grateful for your faith in this.

Also, everybody whom I contacted about the original idea was critical in shaping the end result: Daniel Bogan, Mandy Brown, Jack Cheng, David Cole, Liz Danzico, Chris Fahey, Diana Kimball, Cassie McDaniel, Timothy Meaney, Derek Moore, Mig Reyes, Ricky Salsberry, Jason Schwartz, Justin Skolnick, Erin Watson, and Carolyn Wood.

Joseph Mohan provided advice on the printing process, Jana Kinsman drew the authors, Katherine Walker gave feedback about the cover, and Kaitlyn Tierney copyedited.

And finally, my family and girlfriend have been tremendously supportive through all of my endeavors. This one's for them.

[Information] creates a need for propaganda in man, which in turn opens the door to psychic aggressions and to sentimental, political seductions. Once again, let us refrain from erecting the kind of Manichean world that propaganda suggests – one side white, the other black, a good side, a bad side – saintly information, on the one hand, diabolical propaganda, on the other. The truth about the devil is that he created ambiguity.

—Jaques Ellul, *Propaganda*

Hard Fun

The Zynga abyss.

by **Benjamin Jackson**
bhjackson@gmail.com, @benjaminjackson

A YOUNG BOY VISITS HIS AILING GRANDMOTHER on her deathbed. She beckons him to her side. *Come close, my boy. I have something to share with you. In my will, I have left you a beautiful homestead with over a thousand acres, covered in orange groves, corn fields, and a flower garden with the rarest and most exotic orchids in the world. Young man, you will inherit the most spectacular plot of land this side of the Pacific Ocean.* 1

The boy stares blankly, unmoved. "Grandma," he says, "I'm done with FarmVille. My friends and I switched to Mafia Wars last summer." 2

In 1769, Wolfgang von Kempelen built a machine to impress Maria Theresa, the queen of Bohemia. Dubbed the *Automaton Chess-Player*, it baffled spectators across the Americas for over eighty years, inspiring an investigative article from 3

Edgar Allen Poe.[1] The machine consisted of a cabinet with a chessboard on top, and playing as an imaginary opponent, it defeated the most skilled human players of the time.

But the machine, more commonly known as 4
the **Mechanical Turk**, was an elaborately constructed ruse: a highly-skilled chess player of extremely small stature was hidden in the cabinet. Openings on the sides revealed gears, levers, and machinery that tricked spectators into thinking that the Baron had devised some mechanical way to intelligently respond to a player's moves.[2]

The Mechanical Turk is an early example 5
of unethical game design.[3] Later examples include Three-Card Monte, in which a spectator is shown a card, is asked to follow it with their eyes, and is misled into following the

---

1. Edgar Allan Poe, "Maelzel's Chess-Player", *Southern Literary Messenger* 2:318-326, Apr 1836. This piece has been reposted in full at http://dsn.tc/01a-01.

2. The Mechanical Turk's impact reached further than Baron von Kempelen could have ever imagined. Over a century after Poe wrote about the hoax, the Turk inspired Alan Turing to write the first computer chess program, which began a line of achievements that led to IBM's Deep Blue, the chess machine that defeated then-world champion Garry Kasparov in 1997. Coverage of this event is available at "Kasparov vs. Deep Blue: The Rematch", *IBM Research*. http://dsn.tc/01a-02.

3. Terry Schenold, "Unethical Game Design & Compulsion Manipulation", *Critical Gaming Project*. http://dsn.tc/01a-03.

wrong card. Many casino games are unethical, too; for example, slot machines usually randomize their payouts to encourage players to keep playing, even when they're clearly losing money.[4] But unethical traits can appear in any game, no matter how subtle, and recent games indicate a fuzzier moral ground.

Penguin Suits, Virtual Crops, and Dead Fish

Social games have emerged that leverage 6
networks of friends – mostly via Facebook – to create **Massively Multiplayer Online Role-Playing Games** (MMORPGs). These games are free to play, but they often include virtual currencies that can be earned in-game or purchased with real money, and they don't encourage players to pay until after they sign up. Examples abound:

- In 2005, New Horizon Interactive, a three- 7
person interactive graphics company, released an MMORPG for ages 6–14 called Club Penguin. It casts players in the role of cartoon penguins, each with their own igloo, who chat with their friends via an *Ultimate Safe Chat* that only allows a list of predetermined "safe" phrases. In addition, players can use "coins", an in-game currency, to decorate their penguins by purchasing clothes,

---

4. A more thorough discussion of slot machines and partial reinforcement can be found in Berstein et al., *Psychology, 9th Edition,* Wadsworth Publishing, 2011, p. 215. http://dsn.tc/01a-04.

accessories, and in-game pets called "puffles". An "allowance" of coins can be purchased by the player's legal guardian for a fixed monthly fee.

- In July 2007, Mark Pincus, a Wharton grad with 8
a background in financial analysis and venture capital, co-founded Zynga, a company that specialized in social gaming on Facebook.[5] In 2009, Zynga released FarmVille, an MMORPG where players are cast as farmers who tend crops on a virtual plot of land. *Farm coins* are used to purchase equipment, although the most valuable currency, *farm cash*, is normally only earned by "leveling up" (reaching an arbitrary level of accomplishment) or completing offers. Farm cash is the only way to buy some items; additional farm cash can be purchased with real money, and farm coins cannot.[6]
- In April of 2010, Mitch Liu and Rizwan Virk co- 9
founded Gameview Studios and released Tap Fish, an app that allows children to maintain their own aquarium. Players are provided with a set of free fish, or they can buy new fish through in-app purchases. Fish can die from neglect if the child hasn't signed on for a while – for

---

5. Since Zynga's inception, the company has purchased many popular casual games with player bases largely outside of Facebook, such as Words With Friends and Drop7.
6. Val Wilson, "Farmville Coins and Cash – What is the Difference?", *Farmville Magic*. http://dsn.tc/01a-05.

example, if they go on a family vacation – but they must then pay to "bring it back to life".

Before we get into the human psychology 10
that underlies these games, a historic example.

Skinner's Box

In the 1890s, while studying natural sciences 27
at Saint Petersburg University,[7] a Russian mathematician named Ivan Pavlov was analyzing dogs' saliva output. Pavlov noticed that dogs tended to salivate more before eating – and that merely the sight of a white lab coat would induce salivation, even if no food was on the way.[8] So he rang a bell before presenting them with food, and found that over time, the dogs would salivate even if a bell was rung with no food presented.

Pavlov's research defined classical con- 28
ditioning, in which a **primary reinforcer**[9] – one which naturally elicits a response, such as food or a small electrical shock – is associated with a conditioned or **secondary reinforcer**, such as the lab coat or bell.

Forty years later, as a young psychologist 29
in graduate school, Burrhus Frederic Skinner built on Pavlov's observations. He constructed a soundproof, lightproof chamber that housed a small animal. A lever or button was placed

---

7. Now called Saint Petersburg State University.
8. Lotta Fredholm, "Pavlov's Dog", *Nobelprize.org*. http://dsn.tc/01a-09.
9. Also known as an *unconditioned stimulus*.

A Brief Glossary

In the interest of reaching the broadest possible 11
audience, I've defined some terms below. If you've been playing video games long enough that you owned an original Nintendo, you can probably skip ahead to the next section.

- **Achievements:** Also known as trophies or 12
challenges, these are meta-goals that are unrelated to the game's main structure. World of Warcraft has explicit "Achievement Points", and later Call of Duty titles acknowledge difficult tasks with awards like "Four of a Kind", which is awarded after performing four "headshot" kills in a row.[1] Leveling up is a specific kind of an achievement.
- **Balance:** Tuning a game's rules to create a level 13
playing field and moderate enough difficulty to keep players from becoming discouraged. For example, a fighting game might seek balance in the abilities of each character in order to prevent severely mismatched gameplay.
- **Behavioral Psychology:** A branch of 14
psychology concerned with the study and alteration of human behavior, including our actions, emotions and thoughts.

---

1. "Call of Duty 4: Modern Warfare Achievements", *xbox360achievements.org*. http://dsn.tc/01a-06.

- **Engagement:** The desire to continue playing the game. Engagement is created when there is enough game balance and novelty that the player is willing to spend the time and effort to achieve mastery. Engagement is maintained by offering a constantly-evolving challenge. 15
- **Experience Points (XPs):** An arbitrary unit of measurement, commonly used in RPGs to measure progress outside of the actual mission. Experience points are usually awarded after completing a goal, overcoming an opponent, or discovering a hidden item. 16
- **First-Person Shooter (FPS):** A style of game in which the player sees through the eyes of a gun-toting hero. Wolfenstein 3D, released in 1992, helped popularize the genre. Other popular titles include Doom, the Quake series, Halo, Half Life, and Counter-Strike. 17
- **Flow:** A mental state of full immersion in a single task. Characterized by feelings of increased focus amidst long periods of uninterrupted activity.[2] 18
- **Freemium:** A business model where a product is offered for free while charging for related features, functionality, or services. Often used to monetize MMORPGs. 19
- **Gamification:** The use of game mechanics in non-game environments to solve problems and engage audiences. Used by companies 20

---

2. For more on flow, see Mihály Csíkszentmihályi, *Flow: The Psychology of Optimal Experience*, Harper Perennial, 1990.

like Weight Watchers, Foursquare, and Stack Overflow to encourage desired behaviors.[3]

- **Leveling Up:** The act of collecting a 21
predetermined number of experience points so that the player reaches a new "level". A type of achievement most often seen in RPGs, leveling up is usually accompanied by an increase in strength or endurance.
- **Mastery:** Comprehensive skill in a game. 22
Acquiring mastery is the subject of much study; for example, Anders Ericsson researched "the 10,000 hour rule" by describing how masterful classical musicians had practiced for 2–3 hours a day for at least ten years.[4]
- **Massively Multiplayer Online Role-Playing 23
Game (MMORPG):** A subgenre of RPGs where a large group of players interact with each other in a virtual world. World of Warcraft, Second Life, and Minecraft are common examples.
- **Replay Value:** The ability for a game to be played 24
more than once. Games with high replay value are generally held in higher regard, as they are considered more "timeless" by reviewers.[5]

---

3. Gamification is sometimes mistakenly used to describe the practice of applying RPG-like elements, like leveling up, to other games. You can only gamify things that aren't already games.
4. Anders Ericsson, "The Making of an Expert", *Harvard Business Review*, Jul 2007. http://dsn.tc/01a-07.
5. Adam Bishop, "The Myth of Replay Value", *Gamasutra*. http://dsn.tc/01a-08.

- **Reward Systems:** Game mechanics that 25
condition a player to respond in a certain way. A classic example: the Goomba from Super Mario Bros. When Mario walks into one, he loses a life. This teaches the player to kill the goombas by jumping on them, rather than to run into them headfirst.
- **Role Playing Game (RPG):** A game in which 26
players assume the roles of characters, and act out a story in a fictional (usually fantasy) setting. The most famous RPG is Dungeons and Dragons; World of Warcraft has dominated online.

within the animal's reach, which triggered a primary reinforcer.[10] Called the **Skinner box**, the device paved the way for a new experimental method, leading to innovations in study design, allowing researchers to determine the relative addictiveness of cocaine in isolation versus in a larger community,[11] and to explore the question of whether rats have empathy.[12]

Skinner is now credited as the father of **operant conditioning**: a form of learning where a subject eventually responds to a secondary reinforcer by associating it with some form of primary reinforcement. Not only did Skinner's work show that associations between primary and secondary reinforcers

---

10. In Skinner's case, the animals were pigeons and the primary reinforcer was a small treat.
11. Bruce K. Alexander's *Rat Park* study used a Skinner box to show that rats will self-administer cocaine in isolation, but will refrain when housed in a larger community. See Bruce K. Alexander, "The Myth of Drug-Induced Addiction", 2001. http://dsn.tc/01a-10.
12. They do, though sometimes male rats take the low road. See also Inbal Ben-Ami Bartal et al., "Empathy and Pro-Social Behavior in Rats", *Science* 334(6061):1427-1430. Also available behind a paywall at http://dsn.tc/01a-11.

appear in nature, it also demonstrated that new reinforcers can be developed.[13]

Skinner and Pavlov both proved that pri- 31
mary reinforcers are extremely powerful motivators. For example, after sex and sleep, bacon is one of nature's most powerful primary reinforcers, partly due to its high fat and protein content in comparison to other meats. Bacon has become known as the *gateway meat*: the smell can trigger intense cravings, even in vegetarians.[14] But in a world where fatty foods are so readily available, our instinctual craving for them can cause significant health problems.[15]

The box also taught us two fundamental 32
lessons, one of which had ramifications that extended far beyond Skinner's experiments. Humans are hardwired to respond to primary reinforcers, just like any other animals. And while

---

13. For proof, ask anyone who's taken a smoking cessation aid and then smoked how the cigarette tasted. Bupropion has a success rate of 27% vs. 11% placebo at 26 weeks. Serena Tonstad, et al., "Bupropion SR for smoking cessation in smokers with cardiovascular disease", *Eur Heart J* 24(10):946-55, May 2003. http://dsn.tc/01a-12.

14. Eliza Barclay, "Why Bacon is a Gateway to Meat for Vegetarians", *NPR*. http://dsn.tc/01a-13.

15. Usually these are called lifestyle illnesses when they result in preventable issues with one's daily routine. For more information on the spread of such problems, see Kate Devlin, "Lifestyle diseases 'on the rise as traditional killers cancer and heart disease decline'", *The Telegraph*, 1 Apr 2010. http://dsn.tc/01a-14.

primary reinforcers have a diminishing effect once we're satiated, secondary reinforcers, like money or social status, exist outside our biological needs, and these never hit a satiation point. In other words: we are hardwired to seek approval from our peers, and we can never get enough of it.

So, many people defend FarmVille as a harm- 33
less distraction, arguing that the thousands of hours spent playing the game would still have been wasted on other activities. But there's no question that the social game market, with its virtual currencies and unlimited stock of goods, is a huge cash cow.[16] And it's also clear, as we'll see shortly, that it was engineered to coerce users into tending their virtual plots of land for as long as possible. But before we go into the details of FarmVille's design, it's worth asking a simple question: are any games really *bad*, beyond just being terribly designed or just plain drudgery?

After all, it's just a game, right? 34

Black, White, and 254 Shades of Gray

Moral relativism aside, I think "bad" games exist 35
– provided we define "bad" in unambiguous terms. In *Groundwork of the Metaphysics of Morals*, Immanuel Kant tried to define this with the **Categorical Imperative**, a set of rules to

---

16. Jeferson Valaderes, "Freemium Mobile Gamers Spend Most Money on Items They Don't Keep", *Flurry Blog*, 16 Aug 2011. http://dsn.tc/01a-15.

gauge the ethical consequences of any action.[17] But regardless of how we choose to evaluate a game's morality, there are certain traits that can push it closer to the "evil" side of the spectrum.

36 The primary characteristic of unethical games is that they are manipulative, misleading, or both. From a user experience standpoint, these games employ **dark patterns**, which are common design decisions that trick users into acting against their will.[18] Dark patterns are usually employed to maximize some metric of success, such as email signups, checkouts, or upgrades; they generally test well when they're released to users.

37 For example, FarmVille, Tap Fish, and Club Penguin play on deep-rooted psychological impulses to make money from their audiences. Here are some of the techniques they use:

- 38 **Completion urge:** Humans have a natural desire to finish what they start. Direct mail marketing companies were among the first to notice this when response rates spiked by adding peel-off stickers and half-finished stories to the covers

---

17. *Groundwork of the Metaphysic of Morals,* Immanuel Kant, 1785. http://dsn.tc/01a-16.

18. See the Dark Patterns Wiki at http://wiki.darkpatterns.org/ for a full list, and Harry Brignull, "Dark Patterns: Deception vs. Honesty in UI Design", *A List Apart,* http://dsn.tc/01a-18 provides a more nuanced discussion of the topic.

of marketing materials.[19] These appealed to our natural tendency to complete unfinished tasks, so we removed the stickers and read the entire story.[20] In gaming, FarmVille prominently displays a progress bar that compels players to "like" the FarmVille page, turn on email notifications, and spam their friends' walls.[21]

- **Partial reinforcement:** Also known as 39
uncertain rewards, the encouragement of repeated play by providing sporadic, randomly-timed rewards. Most social games time their rewards on an uncertain schedule.
- **Avoidance:** The threat of punishment for 40
extended absences from playing. When a player stops playing FarmVille for an extended period of time, their crops wither and die. This plays on humans' natural tendency to avoid negative stimuli, even if it involves repeating dull tasks.[22]

---

19. Because they successfully encourage a behavior that the product's creators desire, dark patterns tend to fare well in usability studies or A/B tests. Many businesses need to make a case against their use in the face of numbers that may indicate positive change on the surface.

20. Edward L. Nash, *Direct Marketing: Strategy, Planning, Execution,* McGraw-Hill, 2000, p. 226. http://dsn.tc/01a-19.

21. Brian Meidell, "STF - What I learned From FarmVille So You Don't Have To Play It". http://dsn.tc/01a-20.

22. The notorious "button" in J.J. Abrams' TV series *Lost* is an interesting example of the avoidance principle in popular culture. See "Pushing the button", *Lostpedia.* http://dsn.tc/01a-21.

In one experiment, rats were placed in a cage with a metal floor that delivered a small shock at 30-second intervals, unless the rats pressed a lever to defer it. The rats quickly learned to press the lever to avoid the negative reinforcer.[23]

- **Reciprocity effect:** Providing generosity before 41
asking for something in return. Members of the International Society for Krishna Consciousness, commonly known as the Hare Krishna movement, often give people free books and ask for donations shortly afterward. FarmVille allows players to send free "gifts" to each other. Friends feel compelled to return the favor, which encourages a virtuous cycle that drives players back to the game.[24]
- **Egotism:** Our natural drive to focus on our 42
own favorable traits. This has been shown to affect our ethical judgements[25] and how we perceive our own work.[26] We're proud of our own accomplishments, and we assume

---

23. Murray Sidman, "Some Notes on 'Bursts' in Free-Operance Avoidance Experiments", *J Exp Anal Behav* 1(2):167-172, Apr 1958. http://dsn.tc/01a-25.
24. Jamie Madigan, "How Reciprocity Yields Bumper Crops in Farmville", *The Psychology of Video Games*, 18 Jan 2010. http://dsn.tc/01a-26.
25. N. Epley and E.M. Caruso, "Egocentric ethics", *Social Justice Research* 17: 171-187, 2004. http://dsn.tc/01a-24.
26. E.M. Caruso et al., "The costs and benefits of undoing egocentric responsibility assessments in groups", *Journal of Personality and Social Psychology* 91: 857-871, 2004. http://dsn.tc/01a-47.

that others are deeply interested in our lives. Social games take advantage of this by frequently providing opportunities to share our in-game activities with our friends.

This trend is not just limited to social 43
games, though. Many combat games, like America's Army, serve as thinly-veiled recruitment tools for the U.S. Military.[27] Some brands have launched Facebook games, such as Cheez-It's Swap-It!,[28] as tools to sell more products. Both of these games employ dark patterns (or, at best, vapid marketing); they can be used in any sort of game, in any context.

Of course, not all games fall neatly into a clear 44
division between good and evil. "Good" games can ask little in the way of critical thinking and problem solving, but still be fulfilling by your own standards. Tetris is a complex, enriching game that is just as addictive today as when it debuted in 1988, but many would argue that it lacks the problem-solving challenges or rich plots that make adventure games like Sword & Sworcery and The Legend of Zelda so compelling. Different people find meaning and fulfillment in different

---

27. China has developed their own version where the enemies are American soldiers: see "Gamers Target U.S. Troops in Chinese Military 'Shooter'", *Wired*, 17 May 2011. http://dsn.tc/01a-22.

28. Swap-It! has since been taken down, but you can see a demonstration of it at Blockdot, "Cheez-It Facebook Game Swap-It", *YouTube*. http://dsn.tc/01a-23.

aspects of gameplay; that's what makes gaming so fun for players and game designers.

Hard Fun

One of the best-selling independent iOS games[29] 45
is a side-scrolling jumper called Canabalt. It consists of a tiny man running over the rooftops of a dystopian cityscape. Players tap to jump, and the scrolling quickens over time. There is no end to Canabalt, only longer runs; the longest run yet recorded, at 8 minutes and 16 seconds, takes the player through more than 22km of crumbling buildings and falling obstacles.[30]

At IndieCade in October 2011, Adam 46
Saltsman, Canabalt's creator, discussed the notion of *time until death*. All of us have a finite amount of time on earth, and any time we spend on a particular activity is time that we can't spend doing something else. This means that the time we spend gaming represents most of a game's cost of ownership, far more than any money that we spend. If we found that time enjoyable (or rather, if its benefits outweigh its costs), then the game was worth our time.

---

29. The app, released in late 2009, sold over 225,000 copies at the relatively expensive $2.99 price tier before being open-sourced at the close of 2010. "Over $25,000 Raised For Charity: Canabalt Goes Open Source!", *SemiSecret Blog*, 30 Dec 2010. http://dsn.tc/01a-27.

30. Ibrahim Kaluzny, "Canabalt Record 22317m, 2009–09–14, complete run", *YouTube*. http://dsn.tc/01a-28.

Gaming value is subjective, of course, but 47
it's often created by modulating a game's difficulty until players achieve mastery. In a panel at Seattle's CasualConnect in 2011, game designer and consultant Nicole Lazzaro described two types of fun: **easy fun** and **hard fun.**[31] Games that don't challenge players beyond a certain point – "easy fun" – will never allow them to achieve mastery, which could deprive them of a highly rewarding part of playing. On the other hand, "hard fun" demands something of us, and can provide a more worthwhile experience.

The panel also included Demetri Detsaridis, 48
the general manager of Zynga's New York office. Zynga has its own ideas of what constitutes the "real fun" in FarmVille and similar games, and these ideas align with the company's business interests. His answer of how they approach "easy" vs. "hard" fun was telling:

> You know, while we don't necessarily have this framework in particular in mind... you know, while I was looking at this chart yesterday, while we were talking, I was thinking "Well, Zynga does a lot, if not most, of its development work in this kind of infinity symbol loop here between 'people' fun and 'easy' fun... there's sort of an overlap here that isn't maybe entirely clear on the chart, but a lot of... I think a lot of

31. Margaret Wallace, "Your Brain on Games: The Hidden Psychology of Gaming", *CasualConnect*. http://dsn.tc/01a-30.

> social games kind of are really quite close to the top, you know three-quarters of this, that the 'people' fun and the 'easy' fun are really sort of mushed together, and that where you see the hard fun coming in is in perhaps surprising places, like thinking about your social graph and how you, in real life, are managing that – well, am I sending, you know, friend requests to these, these people? Is that – you know, so that's actually part of the game, and designers know that, so that sort of is an interesting almost meta-game layer of almost 'hard' fun on top of what otherwise might seem in this structure to be really people- and easy-centric.

Detsardis nodded in approval as Rob Tercek, the panel's moderator, summed it up:

> The games themselves aren't where the action happens; the strategy component is: when do you reach out into your social graph? When are you going to spam that list? How frequently are you gonna do that?

I'll reiterate this in plainer language, just in case the quote wasn't clear: Detsaridis said that one of the most compelling parts of playing Zynga's games is deciding when and how to spam your friends with reminders to play Zynga's games.

Creating hard fun isn't an easy task. It requires thinking deeply about the gamer's experience, not just using cheap tricks to drive engagement. FarmVille, Tap Fish, and

Club Penguin all employ Skinner-like techniques to persuade people to spend more time and money. But there are plenty of honest ways to create real engagement, and it's our responsibility as creators and consumers of games to demand more honest and fulfilling fun from our entertainment.

We've established that many games take 50
behavioral shortcuts to drive engagement, but to play devil's advocate, one might make the argument that these games have some redeeming qualities – even if they don't extend much further than art direction and character design. So if we're to argue that a fully "evil" game might exist, it begs the question: *what would such a game look like?*

The Worst Game Ever Made

Described by Wired as "a borderline-evil 51
piece of work that was intended to embody the worst aspects of the modern gaming industry", Ian Bogost's game Cow Clicker, released in 2010, was first intended as a joke:[32]

> The rules were simple to the point of absurdity: There was a picture of a cow, which players were allowed to click once every six hours. Each time they did, they received one point, called a click. Players could invite as many as eight friends to join their "pasture";

32. Jason Tanz, "The Curse of Cow Clicker: How a Cheeky Satire Became a Videogame Hit", *Wired*, 20 Dec 2011. http://dsn.tc/01a-29.

> whenever anyone within the pasture clicked their cow, they all received a click. A leaderboard tracked the game's most prodigious clickers. Players could purchase in-game currency, called mooney, which they could use to buy more cows or circumvent the time restriction. In true FarmVille fashion, whenever a player clicked a cow, an announcement – "I'm clicking a cow" – appeared on their Facebook newsfeed.

Instead, he became trapped in an existential nightmare for 18 months. Within two months, the game grew to 50,000 players; many, but not all, were in on the joke. Cow Clicker was conceived as an insult to players of massive social games, but it turned out to be surprisingly addictive. In fact, by most accounts, it appears to have been fairly enjoyable. What it lacked in gameplay variation, it made up for with the same kinds of dark patterns that Zynga uses to encourage players to return:[33] 52

> Bogost kept his players hooked by introducing new cows for them to purchase using virtual mooney or real money. They ranged from the crowd-pleasingly topical (a cow covered in oil and sporting a BP-esque logo on its rump) to the aggressively cynical (the Stargrazer Cow, which was just the original cow facing the opposite direction and for which Bogost charged 2,500 mooney).

33. *Ibid.*

Nick Yee, a researcher at PARC, offered a solid explanation for the game's success:[34]

> [Yee] says that good games usually offer meaningful opportunities for achievement, social interaction, and challenge; otherwise, players become little more than rats in a Skinner box, hitting a button to get a jolt of reinforcement. "The scary thing about Cow Clicker is that it's just an incredibly clear Skinner box," Yee says. "What does that say about the human psyche and how easy it is to seduce us?"

It's safe to say that Cow Clicker is an unethical game. And it might be fine to criticize games for these shady tactics, but it's of little use without pointing out a way forward. To what standards do we hold games, and their creators, when they walk the line between harmless fun and deliberate manipulation? To answer this, we need to explore some of gaming's most universal traits.

Moving the Goal Posts

Gaming is frequently most enjoyable when it has high **replay value**. Chess, for example, is a game with extremely high replay value, with over 10^{123} permutations.[35] Partially because chess has a high replay value, it's

34. *Ibid.*
35. Claude Shannon, "Programming a Computer for Playing Chess", *Philosophical Magazine* Ser.7 41(314), 1950. http://dsn.tc/01a-31.

remained popular for over 1,500 years, even when played against a computer opponent.[36]

54 Games have long employed various techniques to increase their replay value. For example, racing games have time trials with ghost cars, and "battle modes" that pit two players against each other; fighting games and first-person shooters have varying levels of difficulty; platform games have "survival modes" that test how long the player can stay alive on a particular level.

55 But replay value doesn't matter without **balance**: the careful tuning of game mechanics to ensure a fair contest. Balanced games consistently offer a range of options to players, all of which exhibit **fairness**: there are many ways to win, but the outcome is a toss-up, with neither player gaining an unfair advantage.[37]

56 Tic-Tac-Toe is an example of an unbalanced game. A novice will be quickly dispatched by any competent player. And once the logic of the game is revealed, it ceases to have any entertainment value, as the tiny number of variations can easily be committed to memory.

---

36. One could have created a mechanical Tic-Tac-Toe player at the time of the Mechanical Turk – but because Tic-Tac-Toe is so easy to solve, it would hardly have had the same impact. Chess is a classic example of a game with both balance and replay value, partly due to the number of possible outcomes.

37. David Sirlin, "Balancing Multiplayer Games, Part 1: Definitions". http://dsn.tc/01a-32.

Any pair of moderately experienced players will force any Tic-Tac-Toe game to a draw.

57 Pong, on the other hand, is an extremely balanced game. A novice can pick up the controls in a few moments, and the ball moves slowly at first while they get the hang of it. So not only is it easy to learn, but it's fair, too: no player is able to hit the ball faster than another.[38]

58 Balance can often be manipulated by the player, against both the AI and a human opponent. It can also be manipulated by the game designer, either to make the game mirror reality (e.g. the "Rage Meter" in Mortal Kombat vs. DC Universe[39]) or as a deliberate crutch. Take, for example, the infamous "Rubber Band A.I.":[40]

> A hypothetical: You're playing John Madden Football. Your team is up by 13, there's three and a half minutes left until the end of the game, and you have the ball. Your victory is assured, right?

---

38. This helps explain Pong's immense popularity: during its existence, it consistently drew four times as much revenue as other coin-operated machines. See also Steven Kent, "The King and Court", *Ultimate History of Video Games*, Three Rivers Press, 2001, pp. 53–54.
39. Mortal Kombat Wiki, "Rage Meter". http://dsn.tc/01a-34.
40. TV Tropes Wiki, "Rubber Band A.I." http://dsn.tc/01a-33.

> Wrong, because suddenly the AI is twice as fast as you, knows what play you're going to run, and shuts down your offense, forcing you to punt - or, worse, your running back with a high "Hands" rating fumbles the ball, or an AI defensive back makes a miracle interception. On their drive, the AI marches downfield with no difficulty by completing several consecutive bombs, scoring an easy touchdown. Rinse and repeat, and before you know it you've lost what you thought was a safe lead. The video game has just experienced a Miracle Rally.[41]

Balanced games consistently reward players as their skills increase, and discourage others from obtaining an unfair advantage. Games that encourage cheating – or which cheat themselves – do a disservice to their audiences by upending their own balance.

---

41. TV Tropes Wiki, "Miracle Rally". http://dsn.tc/01a-36:

    A pre-requisite of sporting flicks, where the competitor or team… seems to be on their way down, until a pivotal moment happens (often a case of *Put Me In, Coach!*), after which the team stages, yes, a miraculous comeback ending in victory.

    Miracle rallies are common among video games; one example is Mario Kart 64, where computerized opponents become considerably faster in the final seconds of a race. They don't frequently happen in real life, though, and using them in a game is unrealistic.

Many recent games have tried to create the 59
illusion of replay value. FarmVille, Tap Fish, and Club Penguin all use Skinner's work to persuade people to play for longer, which generates more income for the developers. They also allow players to pay to adjust the difficulty level, but in practice this fosters an environment where one succeeds if they pay the most – and even then, there's no technical end to the game.

But why mention this when companies like 60
Zynga aren't doing anything illegal? Aren't they free to make whatever they'd like? Let's take a look at how the legal system deals with the use of behavioral psychology to manipulate consumers.

Ballerina Dolls Don't Dance

There's plenty of precedent for government 61
restriction of the unethical use of psychological techniques. The advertising industry's history is littered with sleazy tactics that play on our weaknesses. For example, the tobacco industry has frequently ignored the harmful effects of their products. Cigarettes are often promoted with images of healthy people, and actors and actresses frequently smoked, providing sex appeal. And junk food companies have long associated their products with fun cartoon characters (e.g. Tony the Tiger, Count Chocula, Chester Cheetah) that create a bond with young consumers. Kellogg's tries to depict Frosted Flakes as the basis of a healthy lifestyle,

when a large bowl of sugar-coated cereal every morning is probably not the quickest way to a flat stomach and a healthy heart.[42]

Lawmakers eventually caught on, and many 62
dishonest tactics have been legislated out of existence. Congress has banned the marketing of tobacco and alcohol to minors, and in June 2009 it extended that ban to include cloves and flavored cigarettes. The Better Business Bureau was established in 1912 to deal with "snake oil" scams in the medical industry, after a federal lawsuit against the Coca-Cola company failed to compel them to remove caffeine from their product.[43] Locally, some cities require chain restaurants to display calorie counts next to menu items.[44]

The FTC has a 23-page document detail- 63
ing the guidelines for advertising to children.[45] The document is worth reading for the hilarious subheadings alone, but for the sake of brevity, I'll quote one of their guidelines, *Ballerina*

---

42. They even depicted Tony riding a horse and racing against cowboys. See Stapuff, "Tony the Tiger rides a horse", *YouTube*. http://dsn.tc/01a-38.

43. Ludy T. Benjamin, "Pop psychology: The man who saved Coca-Cola", *Monitor on Psychology* 40(2):18, Feb 2009. http://dsn.tc/01a-37.

44. "New York's calorie counting", *The Economist*, 28 Jul 2011. http://dsn.tc/01a-35.

45. Federal Trade Commission, "Advertising to Kids and the FTC: A Regulatory Retrospective That Advises the Present", *FTC.gov*. http://dsn.tc/01a-40.

Dolls Don't Dance, Toy Horses Can't Stand Up, and Bread Doesn't Help with Homework:

> During the past three decades, the Commission has brought a number of cases challenging deceptive performance claims in toy advertisements. For example, a ballerina doll was shown to pirouette on one toe unassisted in a TV ad; however, she could not perform in the playroom.
>
> Toy helicopters were depicted on TV as flying and hovering in mid air; in reality, the helicopters were suspended by monofilament wires attached to poles and manipulated by unseen people. A horse named "Nugget" was shown standing on his own; in fact, "Nugget" fell over without human assistance. In each of these cases, the ad was examined from the viewpoint of a child in the age group to which the toy was targeted. While an adult viewer might understand that special techniques were employed in such commercials, the child would expect the toy to perform as shown.

Someday, our government might take a look 64
at the mechanics of games like FarmVille, Tap Fish, and their competitors. In time, their manipulative intent might become clearer. Their virtual – and hence unregulated – currencies are a legal minefield, but in a bizarrely poetic coincidence, they may fall under the same gambling laws that regulate slot machines: perhaps the most profitable Skinner box of

all time.[46] While Congress has usually been slow to enact such regulations, this day might come sooner then we think, especially if others echo the complaints of Frank Mendez:[47]

> Frank Mendez told a local NBC affiliate that he downloaded the free Tap Fish iPhone application for his 7-year-old to play with. The aquarium game allows kids to clean the tank, feed the fish and more. What Mendez didn't realize is that the free app also includes "in-app purchases," which allows users to purchase fish and other virtual items.
>
> So imagine his surprise after opening his May debit card bill and finding charge after charge for "bundles" of fish totaling $613. "I'm aware I have to pay for that, but I think they're taking advantage of the innocence of the kid," Mendez told NBC.

The Daily Show picked this story up, and interviewed Rizwan Virk, one of Tap Fish's founders. They skewered the game's misleading user experience by interviewing a family that

46. Ed Sperling, "Regulating Virtual Currency", *Forbes*, 15 Apr 2010. http://dsn.tc/01a-44.
47. Jorgen Wouters, "Child takes iPhone's 'Tap Fish' bait, reels in $600-plus bill", *Daily Finance*, 7 Dec 2010. http://dsn.tc/01a-43.

spent over $1,500 on the game, and asked Virk how mortal fish can be "revived" for money:[48]

> Interviewer: "So that's a good lesson for kids. If you kill something, you can throw money at it to bring it back to life."
>
> Virk: "Well, that's how the game works."

To be fair, the interview was cut for dramatic effect, and Virk responded on his blog with a lengthy rebuttal of some (but not all) of the show's criticisms.[49] And while a $1,500 expenditure isn't common, other similar incidents have occurred.[50] If stories like Frank's continue to make headlines, these companies will be subjected to the same system of punishment that they employ in their games. If history has revealed one effective way to prevent businesses from tricking their customers, it's to make the offending practices illegal, and punish them until they stop.

---

48. Kirk Hamilton, "The Daily Show Gleefully Rips Into Free-To-Play Gaming", *Kotaku*, 9 Dec 2011. http://dsn.tc/01a-45.
49. Rizwan Virk, "Top 10 Things the Daily Show with Jon Stewart Got Wrong about Tap Fish!", *Zentrepreneur*, 9 Dec 2011. http://dsn.tc/01a-46.
50. Kevin Tofel, "My iTunes Account Was Hacked for $375 – By My Own Kids", *Bloomberg Businessweek*, 8 Jul 2010. http://dsn.tc/01a-42.

Educating the Sharecroppers

In a Harvard University Press blog post on the Mechanical Turk's history, the editors observed that the device represented something larger than just a simple hoax:[51] 65

> Kang notes that the significance of the Turk "points not to the celebration of the mechanical, as in the works of the previous decades, *but precisely the disillusionment with it in the larger culture,*" a disillusionment that Kang takes to mark not just the end of "the automaton craze" but also a significant development in the era's political thought.

If we take history at face value, we're wit- 66
nessing the birth of a new craze, where an obsession with virtual cash and cartoon penguins has replaced our ancestors' fascination with space exploration, self-directing machinery, and the race towards artificial intelligence. The creators of these games are reaping billions of dollars every year, from a modern day Mechanical Turk. But rather than fool us with a physical illusion, they tap into our subconscious and measure every possible way to maximize revenue.

There is hope, however. The Turk had its 67
day, but it was eventually exposed as a cheap parlor trick. If we evaluate games with more than quantitative ratings – if we examine

51. "The Mechanical Turk", *Harvard University Press Blog.* http://dsn.tc/01a-41. Emphasis added.

them closely, and look past their spinning gears and whirring motors into how they truly work – we might look back at the 21st century and tell our children about what we used to play, before we all knew better.

What Designers Know

Keeping research pervasive.

by **Jon Whipple**
jon@jonwhipple.com, @Jon_Whipple

I'M ALWAYS SURPRISED BY HOW MANY THINGS WE KNOW. We train keyboard shortcuts into our muscle memory. We continually learn tips, tricks, and insights from bosses, mentors, and colleagues. Instructors drill ideas into us at school. Over time, we cultivate taste: we know what looks cool and what doesn't. We know how to persuade people and garner attention. We can help people remember things. We can sell toasters. And the things we know aren't limited to what we've been taught – we also know what we've read, recorded, and experienced. We've seen great ideas succeed and fail. We remember the expressions on people's faces when they first see our work. We've learned the right way to present our work, and the right people to present it to. 1

Strange, then, that we always begin our projects with a research phase, as if we know nothing, as if the problem hasn't existed in some other form, as if the client has all the time and money in the world. To be fair, all projects have unknowns. Nobody likes surprises, and sometimes, 2 research reveals important things that we never knew before. But what about the vast majority of our projects? Or the vast majority of the problems that we solve within a project? I'll wager you or your colleagues have seen these problems before – and there's a fair chance that the solution is documented elsewhere in some form.

If research is budgeted, scheduled, and prop- 3
erly conducted, it can be a tremendously valuable activity. It can provide feedback on all of the things we make. But when research is poorly conducted or poorly applied, it can leave the client with the idea that research is expensive and not worthwhile, and that hurts us all in the long run.

Because we already know a great deal, we 4
can move research from a step in the design process to an ongoing, agency-wide activity: we can adopt a **distributed research model**. This model would result in better, more focused work, allowing us to spend more of our energy on specific issues relevant to the project at hand. It would also help us meet deadlines, because we can capitalize on the experience of the designer and community while maintaining a good relationship with the client. In this essay, I'll describe how research is built and distributed across teams, and how it can benefit all of us to focus on institutional knowledge.

The context

I work at a cross-platform agency for web 5
design, print design, corporate identity, and enterprise CMS development. Over the past few years, I've focused on speed in designing for all types of clients. Faster implementation creates something useful today, rather than something perfect tomorrow, while sacrificing as little as possible in quality.

We're a small firm, with a total staff of ten. 6
Given the size of our team and the demands of our clients, projects rarely contain a traditional research phase; instead, "research" becomes an ongoing conversation during design and development. For example, an international manufacturer of wireless devices required specialized websites for their developers and sales partners. Building on our experiences with similar businesses, we created a design that addressed most of their objectives, so we could achieve the site's primary goal in a short timeframe. They were startled by our fast response, but as we took them through our designs, they were pleased with their accuracy and utility. The project led to an opportunity to design their corporate website.

While they expected a research phase with 7
far more preliminary work, we drew from our own personal experience instead. Exhaustive research and analysis were replaced with simple conversations with the client. Our approach would be refined during its implementation,

and even the refinements came from our prior experience. After going through this process a few times now, we've learned a new way of doing things. We trust our existing knowledge and experience, we keep our research and knowledge at the top of our minds[1] as we design, we organize our research so it's easily available to everyone, we structure the company so people collaborate across disciplines, and we keep the client involved through every step.

Before I explain this further, though, a few 8
words on the history of design processes.

The current way: the *Research First Model*

As designers, we usually talk to our clients 9
and colleagues in terms of a **design process**, or a particular way of moving from ideation to execution. It's something that typifies design activity on all kinds of projects, and this practice is taken very seriously. In some cases, organizations value their processes so much that they have even copyrighted or trademarked them.[2]

---

1. More thoughts on this notion are available at Paul Graham, "The Top Idea In Your Mind". http://dsn.tc/01b-01.

2. For example, Landor's process once hinged on its proprietary Brand Driver™. See also Landor, "Capabilities: Brand Driver", *Landor.com*. http://dsn.tc/01b-03.

In *How Do You Design?: A Compendium of Models*,[3] Hugh Dubberly describes over 80 design processes. Many of them are quite similar, usually variations of the 4D model: define, design, develop, and deploy.[4] Indeed, design activity can't take place without some definition of the problem to be solved and how we might go about solving that problem. These parts of the design process are generally covered by research and analysis. 10

In *Generic Work Process Version 1.0*,[5] Bas Leurs et al. define the elements and cycles "...of the methods and techniques which can be used throughout the user-centered design process". The process begins with research and analysis, and progresses through conceptualization, design, development, and implementation. 11

A pattern emerges after enough time. Research plays a part in establishing credibility: it moves design decisions away from personal preferences, easing client relations in the process. Research functions as a lubricant, reducing friction around contentious issues and providing consensus among designers, 12

---

3. Hugh Dubberly, "How Do You Design? A Compendium of Models". http://dsn.tc/01b-04. Also see http://dsn.tc/01b-02 for a range of design processes.
4. For one such example of the 4D model, see "4D: How We Work", *MyProgrammer*. http://dsn.tc/01b-05.
5. Bas Leurs et al., "Generic Work Process". http://dsn.tc/01b-14.

developers, and clients. The upshot is that a clearly defined result, commonly understood facts, and relevant data make design discussions easier. Project stakeholders can move from debates of *personal preference* to decisions based on *comprehensive understanding*.

The **Research First Model** is based on several 13
assumptions:

1. **We're confronting a unique problem.** We 14
may confront problems that are unique to us, because we haven't yet been asked to solve them in our own careers. But most problems have probably already been addressed by someone else. The fact that we may not be able to find an existing example doesn't necessarily prove this assumption true, as it's hard to know the things that we don't know.[6]
2. **There are many unknowns for both client and** 15
designer. In this case, people think the problem domain is so unfamiliar that undiscovered information will have a critical bearing on the project's outcome. Although it may be true that something unknown could change the

6. This leads to a phenomenon known as the *Dunning-Kruger effect*. For more on this, see Errol Morris, "The Anosognosic's Dilemma: Something's Wrong But You'll Never Know What It Is (Part 1)", *The New York Times*, 20 Jun 2010. http://dsn.tc/01b-06.

solution, this represents the exception, not the rule. For the vast majority of problems, the broad approach has already been discovered.

Design patterns help address this.[7] For ex- 16
ample, if the user needs to "view data items from a potentially large set of sorted data that will not be easy to display within a single page", we can display that list across several pages by implementing *pagination*.[8] If the "user wants to find or submit a particular piece of information based on a date or between a date range", we can provide a *calendar picker*. We might need to change the way these patterns are implemented, but they provide us with a solid foundation. In situations where there doesn't seem to be an existing pattern, it's best to finish applying patterns in other parts of the project, and then return to the original problem and work on a customized solution in context.

3. **We design in a vacuum.** Design has no value 17
outside a context of business requirements. We often discover that a client has many processes

---

7. Pattern libraries are a collection of repeatable solutions to common design problems. Inspired by the framework set forth in architect Christopher Alexander's *A Pattern Language* and *The Timeless Way of Building* (Oxford University Press), design patterns can apply to programming (Erich Gamma et al., *Design Patterns*, Addison-Wesley, 1994), user experience design (Jennifer Tidwell, *Designing Interfaces*, O'Reilly, 2006), and many other fields.

8. Yahoo!, *YUI Pattern Library*. http://dsn.tc/01b-08.

that work against a design solution; or that their organization is factional, persistently infighting. The project changes because the problems gain clarity, and suddenly we're consulting on issues far more broad than the design of only one thing. When a project's resolution acts as a "pipeline to your corporate soul",[9] designers grapple with far broader questions.

4. **No previous research has occurred for this type of problem.** Design process has been an area of study since the 1920s, and the subject of significant interest since WWII.[10] Interest in HCI and UX has existed for as long as computing itself.[11] The Web led to an explosion of research around what we practice. Common interactions adopt common, useful, and effective solutions. Through repeatedly applying these solutions, they become subtly refined over time. We don't need to conduct any cognitive science research to discover them; all we need to do is figure out what's been done before, and

---

9. Alan Cooper, "The pipeline to your corporate soul", *Cooper Blog*, 20 Sep 2011. http://dsn.tc/01b-07.
10. Vannevar Bush, "As We May Think", *The Atlantic*, Jul 1945. http://dsn.tc/01b-09.
11. For example, Richard Saul Wurman coined the term "information architecture" in 1974, almost a decade before the introduction of the personal computer. See also "Richard Saul Wurman: The InfoDesign Interview". http://dsn.tc/01b-10.

adapt it to the problem at hand. And along the way, we may find ways to improve them.

5. **There is enough time and money to conduct** 19
research. When it comes to institutionalizing research, an agency is its own worst enemy. Agencies emphasize research when upper management creates the budget for it. Likewise, if clients believe they need to focus on research, they'll choose a research-focused agency. Freelancers or small boutiques may not be able to justify this cost, or they may not be able to successfully sell research to their clients.
6. **There are enough qualified interview subjects** 20
to conduct research. Even if there's enough time and money for a formal research project, there may not be enough help from the target audience. This assumption is based on the existence of enough qualified, easy-to-find participants who can be guided by an experienced professional. Recruiting qualified researchers and participants can be difficult, especially for small firms.[12] In situations with tight timelines and poor

---

12. The best participants for these studies have rarely, if ever, participated in one already, so they can use a product with few preconceptions about its utility. Fortunately, tools now exist that try to find a way around this problem, such as Bolt|Peters's "Ethnio": http://ethn.io.

resources, this issue can be circumvented through guerrilla-style research techniques.[13]

7. **We can know everything relevant there is** 21
to know about the problem. This assumption justifies most research effort: the idea that we can discover and analyze all of a project's relevant information. Though reassuring, this is a dangerous line of thinking that chases an impossibility. How do we ever know when we know "enough"? Horace Dediu refers to this as the **Analyst's Paradox.**[14] Research is required, of course, and more research can lead to better analysis and decision. However, more research also means more time and money are expended before we can take action. At some point, we must always base our recommendations on a degree of informed intuition. Where do we draw the line?

Over the course of my career, I've seen 22
many ways that the Research First model has worked against us. In one such instance, a client asked us to redevelop their content management system with customer-facing web pages

---

13. See also Cennydd Bowles and James Box, *Undercover User Experience Design,* New Riders, 2010; Jakob Nielsen, "Guerilla HCI", *useit.com,* http://dsn.tc/01b-13; Jakob Nielsen, "Discount Usability: 20 Years", *useit.com,* http://dsn.tc/01b-12; and Todd Zaki Warfel, *Prototyping,* Rosenfeld Media, 2009.

14. Horace Dediu, "Episode 12: Back to the Future", *The Critical Path,* 7:01 http://dsn.tc/01b-16.

that would be designed by a partner agency. The project repeatedly stalled, as both the client and my firm waited for the agency to conduct re search and create UX deliverables. While waiting, we restructured the CMS and familiarized ourselves with the existing content model, so we could determine how it could be modified.

As the other agency generated content re- 23
quirements and wireframes for each type of page, we also called the client's sales team and listened to the frustrations that they and their prospects currently faced. This simple act of "research" was really just a practical conversation, and it resulted in a lot of useful knowledge that we shared in team-wide meetings. We used our research to critique the other agency's work, both confirming good ideas and pointing out problem areas. Surprised by our feedback, they frequently requested extra time to revise their work.

Subsequent meetings confirmed our previous 24
discoveries. When the client finally approved our work, they provided the caveat that subsequent visual design would be subject to significant time constraints, which heavily narrowed our scope in the interest of meeting our deadline: hardly the outcome we meant to obtain.

In this example, of the seven assumptions 25
that I previously outlined, *all of them* were disproven.

- *The problems confronting the client were not* 26
  unique. They wanted to make it easier for
  their customers to get the right information
  about their software. This is a common
  problem in our field, and I'm sure the
  design team had experienced it in similar
  forms. In fact, their organization ostensibly
  exists to address this very problem.
- *There weren't many unknowns.* The sales team 27
  already knew most of the problems, and had
  relayed the information to other team members.
  This was clarified in phone conversations,
  where we discovered a disconnect between
  what users expected and what they experienced.
  Meanwhile, the design team contacted some
  of our client's customers to find out about their
  experiences. Despite translating through the
  sales team, we had more accurate information
  than the other agency's team did, and because
  we frequently shared our findings with each
  other, we were able to act on them more quickly.
- *The design team's research didn't help* 28
  when it became apparent that our
  client faced internal criticism. This was
  compounded by the short timeline that
  the client's executives had established.
- *In fact, previous research had already occurred.* 29
  How do you connect prospective customers
  with useful information? What does the
  prospect need to know before they speak
  with you? What do you want them to know

that makes your product more compelling than that of your competitors? Surely these questions have been answered before, and the other agency's designers must have confronted them regularly with other clients.[15]

- *There wasn't enough time, money, or participants* 30
  to create quality research. Assumptions 5 and 6 became problematic when the design team requested more time for research and analysis, even when the rest of the project was behind schedule. The client was already convinced that the problem had been defined, and they believed that we had sufficient information from our interviews.
- *Finally, the design team couldn't comprehensively* 31
  understand all of the problems that the sales team confronted. Again, substantial information was already available through previous conversations. Although our information wasn't entirely precise, it was useful enough to act on before the project's deadline.

✤

This experience isn't unique. I've disproven 32
these seven assumptions in many different circumstances, across many kinds of project. Time after time, deploying a proven

---

15. We certainly had, and we were able to suggest solutions and patterns that we had used before.

pattern for a particular problem, asking questions, and comparing findings with known examples has resulted in effective, useful, economical solutions that provide robust foundations for a project's future.

A New Approach: the *Distributed Research Model*

Knowing all of this, I propose a new way of 33
working in an agency: the **Distributed Research Model**. Distributing research throughout an organization provides it with a cultural identity that can set a strong precedent for the future, while aiding its capability to solve common problems. Mule Design's Mike Monteiro describes a similar model:[16]

> We don't do research before we start designing, we do research as *part* of designing. This is an integral part of the design process. It cannot be taken away, otherwise you have not designed anything.

Even without dedicated research staff, we have consistently benefited from the following values:

- *Always research.* Keep your radar on. Record and 34
share the details of every story, essay, article, and book that you encounter. This builds internal knowledge that more forcefully informs future decisions. Spreading that knowledge also ensures a broader understanding of any research activity.

---

16. From the podcast Let's Make Mistakes, "Episode 3: Making Things for People", 13:20. Recording available at http://dsn.tc/01b-15.

- *Always experiment.* We try new things as often as possible. We try new design tools, prototyping techniques, visual effects, and programming methods. Sometimes we abandon them because they aren't a natural fit at the time, but we always leave the door open to revisit them later. Either way, the results are treated as internal research, and they become part of the firm's general knowledge. 35
- *Conduct multiple activities at once.* Be wary of projects that don't allow you to conduct multiple activities at the same time. If a "waterfall" project's steps contain all previous steps as prerequisite, it probably isn't the most efficient use of your time and effort. Not only can this impair your speed of delivery, it also makes the project harder to mine for research. 36
- *Try to create something that is useful now.* If knowledge is widespread in your organization, it builds closer relationships that allow you to work more quickly without second-guessing each other as often. Working quickly allows smaller iterations, which provide more flexibility if things aren't working. It also places your client in a posture of action: they're primed to respond to ongoing work, and encouraged to keep up with the project's momentum, with greater focus on what work needs to be done. 37
- *Sacrifice the project's scope if needed.* Rather than sacrifice quality under tight timelines or small budgets, we narrow the project's 38

scope and adapt any previous work to solve the new set of problems. Usually, narrowing the scope identifies the core problems that must be immediately addressed. But we do this with an eye to the future, so the client has a useful starting point for incorporating the rest of the features at a later time.

- *There is no spoon.* Design processes are flexible, 39
  and precedent shouldn't set them in stone. Take the time to occasionally reevaluate how you work together. Don't be slaves to any process that takes too long and imperils the project's budget.

Research helps everyone

Research can have many consequences beyond 40
its ability to influence design decisions, and sometimes our research benefits people in other roles more than our designers.

- *Project managers* benefit from all agency 41
  activity if they treat it as research. Any progress on the project – good or bad – provides internal research that people can reference for future similar projects.[17]
- *Salespeople, principals, and planners* can 42
  compare the agency's patterns of income and expenditure, pointing out where costs are focused in order to manage potential issues before they become harder to handle.

---

17. We don't have dedicated project managers in my firm, so our team leaders and client contacts collect and distribute our research instead.

They can also get a sense of whether new prospects are exhibiting the same kinds of "symptoms" as existing problematic clients.

- *Account managers* could research opportunities 43 for follow-up projects and refinements after a project has been finished. This applies to all manner of communications, including refining or supplementing publications, or adding additional features to previously launched websites. Ongoing relationships are based on chains of incremental improvements over a long period of time.
- *Developers* can benefit from research as well. 44 For example, in our work for a global enterprise software company, the conversations we had with their sales and technical teams provided crucial insights for the information architecture, user experience design, and visual design that would follow.

Caveats

This approach doesn't prohibit research: 45 it simply generalizes it, and tries to spread internal knowledge as widely as possible. Instead of making research a discrete step, we need a pervasive culture of research.

You still need to discover what problem 46 you're going to solve. But your experience and general knowledge can serve you well; research can be simple, limited in scope, and far more economical than we commonly perceive it to be.

Concluding thoughts

Research works at its best as a pervasive, 47
ongoing, and informal effort. Research is useful and appropriate in small, focused doses, when it ceases to be a phase in and of itself. This builds client confidence, which in turn developes a thoughtful, practical reputation for yourself.

✤

The Distributed Research model is: 48

- **Pervasive.** Research must happen in every 49
area of the company. Everyone has something valuable to share.
- **Fast.** Research should be handled frequently and 50
incrementally; don't let it pile up. Both you and your client will feel more confident if you make research a routine action.[18]
- **Repeatable.** By generalizing the process to any 51
kind of information and any team member, it's easy to accumulate a lot of knowledge.
- **Catalogued.** On the other hand, it's possible to 52
have too much knowledge. Eventually, enough research builds up that it needs to be categorized and curated if it's going to be of any use.

---

18. Don Norman corroborates this point in his Core77 essay "Act First, Do the Research Later," *Core77.com,* 1 Aug 2011, http://dsn.tc/01b-17; and in "Why doing user observations first is wrong," *jnd.org,* http://dsn.tc/01b-18.

To spread research with the client's inter- 53
ests in mind, your business processes have to be flexible. But we've found that clients are happy, even relieved, to move at our speed, because we can quickly provide them with useful solutions and they can adopt a more hands-on approach.

My experiences may be different from 54
yours. You may have worked in situations where projects have appropriate budgets or less constrained timelines. If that's true, I congratulate you. See if you can't use some of your time to research more, or to share more of its results across your organization. Increasing internal knowledge will always help a company, and we all stand to benefit from a culture built around sharing and collaboration.

Local Communities In Practice and By Design

New ways to meet each other.

by **Vitorio Miliano**
email_from_distance@vitor.io, @vitor_io

IT'S EARLY OCTOBER 2011, AND IXDA AUSTIN IS HOSTING A HAPPY HOUR. I'm having drinks with forty-some-odd folks from the Austin design community: UX practitioners, graphic designers, usability professionals, and creative directors. The tables at this hip East Austin bar's back patio are full of patrons bearing name tags – and many more, similarly branded, are standing, mingling, talking, and networking, with the occasional trip inside for a refill. The happy hour started at 6, and will include an unscheduled third hour before people start to leave en masse. 1

I've met two newcomers tonight. Jenica Welch is from San Francisco, which she characterizes as having a large enough design community that you can't walk down the street without running into a designer on their way to another event. She's been in Austin for a year, but only discovered the IxDA group recently. This is her first time meeting local designers that she doesn't work with. Georgette Sullivan moved here from 2

Kansas City, which she describes as having a small enough design community that all the Adobe software users have to participate in a single user group, instead of one for each product.

Georgette was looking forward to Austin's 3
larger community. Jenica was surprised by how small and hidden it was. Does Austin exist between these two perspectives? How can the local community have failed to support a new designer for a year? What other issues does our design community face? Does your city have similar problems? How can the situation be improved?

Exploring How Austin's Communities Began

Austin has three primary design communities: 4
the active[1] local chapters of AIGA,[2] IxDA,[3] and UPA.[4] For interaction design, usability and user experience, there is also an STC[5] chapter and a growing content strategy meetup,[6] but no

---

1. I define "active" as having a maintained web site, a responsive organizer, and at least four events a year.
2. AIGA, the professional association for design. Austin: http://www.aigaustin.org/. Parent: http://www.aiga.org/.
3. Interaction Design Association. Austin: http://ixdaaustin.ning.com/. Parent: http://www.ixda.org/.
4. Usability Professionals' Association. Austin: http://www.austinupa.org/. Parent: http://www.upassoc.org/.
5. Society for Technical Communication. Austin: http://www.stcaustin.org/. Parent: http://www.stc.org/.
6. Austin Content: http://dsn.tc/01c-10

other professional chapters.[7] For graphic design, there are Adobe user group chapters[8] and a "design and media" meetup,[9] but no presence beyond these.[10] Web developers have multiple groups, but web-specific designers only have a local Refresh[11] chapter. In this essay, I will analyze the composition and behaviors of the attendees of our local IxDA and UPA chapters.

The aforementioned happy hour paints 5
a rosy picture of a vibrant community that wasn't always so. Agencies have only participated recently, and their support remains tepid. Pentagram has had an Austin office since 1994,[12]

---

7. Such professional chapters include, but are not limited to, UX Book Club, Product Design Guild, ACM SIGCHI, American Society for Information Science and Technology, or the Human Factors and Ergonomics Society.
8. "Search: groups matching Austin", *Adobe.com*. http://dsn.tc/01c-09.
9. Austin Texas Design and Media: http://dsn.tc/01c-11.
10. Other professional organizations without Austin chapters include the Graphic Artists Guild, Society for News Design, Society of Publication Designers, Society for Environmental Graphic Design, and the Chartered Society of Designers.
11. Refresh Austin: http://www.refreshaustin.org/.
12. Jenny Sullivan, *Graphic Design America 3: Portfolios from the Best and Brightest Design Firms from Across the United States*, Rockport Publishers, 2005, 194. http://dsn.tc/01c-13.

Frog Design since 1996.[13] But while Frog has hosted SXSW parties since 2004,[14] they have only actively opened themselves to the local community since September 2011. Razorfish has had an office in Austin since 2005.[15] Possible Worldwide[16] and Adaptive Path have had offices in Austin since 2008, but Adaptive Path's coming-out party wasn't until October 2010.[17]

Independent professional organizations haven't fared well, either. Austin UPA's final meeting was in November 2004.[18] Meanwhile, IxDA's Austin chapter had never before held a meeting; its previous organizer had publicly stated he was only interested in hosting formal presentations organized

13. "frogdesign acquires ZFI, adds to Austin office", *frogdesign*, archived 11 Jun 1998. http://dsn.tc/01c-14.
14. Media firm GSD&M hosted the opening party prior to Frog, according to archived pages. "SXSW Interactive Evening Events", *SXSW*, archived March 29, 2004. http://dsn.tc/01c-15.
15. There were no references to an Austin location prior to the Avenue A merger. "office locations", *Avenue A | Razorfish*, archived 4 Feb 2005. http://dsn.tc/01c-16.
16. Sandra Zaragoza, "Schematic Yesterday, Possible Today", *Austin Business Journal*, 21 Feb 2011. http://dsn.tc/01c-17.
17. "We're Throwing a House Party, Texas Style", *Adaptive Path*, accessed 21 Oct 2011. http://dsn.tc/01c-18.
18. "Austin UPA calendar", *Austin UPA*, archived 5 Jul 2008. http://dsn.tc/01c-19.

by others.[19] A lack of support from both industry and the existing community finally drove people to organize by themselves.

The watershed moment came in January 7
2008, when UI designer and researcher Kyra Edeker, after feeling a "hole" in the community over the past year, hosted a happy hour at a new wine bar on a Monday night and unexpectedly packed the house.[20] One of the attendees was Tori Breitling, a freelance user experience designer who found the turnout galvanizing.[21]

Frustrated with the local IxDA organizer's 8
neglect of the chapter despite multiple entreaties from the community, Breitling launched a

---

19. "Texas IxDers," *IxDA mailing list,* last modified 9 Oct 2007. http://dsn.tc/01c-20.

20. Kyra Edeker, email with the author, 17 Oct 2011: "I emailed ~65 people I knew personally/professionally and also the national IXDA list, the local UPA folks and asked friends at agencies around town to spread the word. I stopped counting people at 65 that night (more than half I didn't know - a coincidence that it was near my list total) and I think everyone was surprised at how many of us there were."

21. Tori Breitling, email correspondence with the author, 26 Sep 2011: "...Kyra organized that mixer at that wine bar, at which gobs of people showed up, which showed me that I wasn't the only one interested in getting the community together."

UX Book Club chapter[22] in November 2008[23] while pursuing remedies through IxDA's board. At the same time, usability researcher Julie Lowe, originally seeking a local mentor, had met with the previous UPA chapter's organizer and elected to take it over, keeping it focused on testing and research.[24] UX designer Amy Jones also saw the community's unmet needs and, spurred on by her manager, announced monthly lunches and a mailing list under the name **Austin UX**, choosing independence over the political battles of existing organizations.

Austin UX's first lunch and mailing list posts came only a few weeks before Breitling's book club announcement. Lowe opened Austin UPA's web site in September 2008, and its first meeting was held in January 2009. Austin's UX Book Club held its first meeting at the end of January

---

22. Tori Breitling, email correspondence with the author, 26 Sep 2011: "I thought, well, here was something I could do for myself and Austin, so I jumped on the bandwagon. There was a very strong response from the community, probably around 50 people signed up in a matter of days."

23. One of the first, #13, within four days of Dave Baty founding the project. "Welcome to UX Book Club!" *UX book Club Wiki*, archived revision from 30 Nov 2008. http://dsn.tc/01c-21.

24. Julie Lowe, email correspondence with the author, 10 Oct 2011: "[Tori Breitling] saw UPA being focused on testing and research and IXDA being about the interaction design. Being aware of the two groups for a while now, I would agree with that."

2009, but IxDA Austin was turned over to Breitling at the end of February. After holding IxDA Austin's first meeting at the end of March, Breitling didn't have the time to manage both and, unable to find a co- or replacement organizer, she shuttered UX Book Club in July 2009.

As IxDA and UPA relaunched, members joined at a rate and number which seemed to reflect the openness of their parent group.[25] UPA grew slowly from its initial 34 members in the first two months, spiking to 67 after its first meeting, and settling into an average of 10 new members a month until they changed over to a new mailing list in July 2010. IxDA grew at more than double UPA's rate: 89 members in its first month, and maintaining an average of 24 new members a month over the same time period. Just over half of UPA's initial membership signed up with IxDA after its launch, and after that, members present on both lists were twice as likely to have joined IxDA first.[26]

---

25. You must be a dues-paying member of the national UPA organization to hold office in a local UPA chapter, whereas IxDA is free and entirely volunteer-run. This almost certainly impacts the potential participation levels of each.

26. Austin UPA Ning membership roster export dated 13 Jul 2010, provided by Julie Lowe, covering 4 Sep 2008 through 12 Jul 2010. IxDA Austin Ning membership roster export, collected by the author with access given by Tori Breitling, dated 26 Dec 2010, covering 27 Feb 2009 through 23 Dec 2010.

Meetings in both groups were irregular and 11
informal: a lot of happy hours and short talks, and the duplication of event types may have gone unnoticed because each group was targeting different segments of the community. I felt this was awkward; surely at least the social events could be coordinated?[27] I also felt there was an unmet need for more formal mentoring, continuing education, and technical practice, none of which were directly supported by IxDA or UPA (and, at this point, I had not yet heard of Austin UX).

Feeling like these professional organiza- 12
tions were lacking in formality, in December 2009 I published an essay[28] proposing a practice workshop for designers, which was patterned after Toastmasters International. In January 2010, the Design Workshop held its first meeting, and I would hold these meetings every two weeks through August 2010.

With the resurgence of community activity, 13
Amy Jones shuttered Austin UX in August 2010. I learned of Austin UX as it was closing and, seeing this as further evidence of the community's

---

27. Whether this was a common feeling remains undetermined: "I never felt the 'fractured nature' of the communities was necessarily a problem, but rather a micro-reflection of the parent group[s]." Tori Breitling, email correspondence with the author, 30 Dec 2011.

28. Vitorio Miliano, "Practice user experience and interaction design with your peers", last modified 12 Jan 2010. http://dsn.tc/01c-22.

fractured nature, I relaunched it as an event calendar to document the meetings of design organizations (and non-design organizations holding design-related events) citywide.[29] It provided the appearance of a cohesive community to visitors and outsiders, but the community, when defined as *organizations holding events and attendees of those events*, doesn't behave this way in practice.

Qualifying Community Membership

Both IxDA Austin and Austin UPA define 14
their "membership" as names on a mailing list. No dues are required to participate, and there is no other barrier to entry. Not all events require RSVPs, so attendees may make up a different segment of the population than those signed up on the organization's lists and websites. Finally, the mechanics of these lists and websites may affect participation.

IxDA Austin is a Ning[30] site containing 15
web-based forums, a calendar, and a broadcast-only mailing list. A "member" is someone who has signed up to receive notices about events, RSVPed to an event, or posted a job

29. http://austinux.org/.

30. "Ning, the World's Largest Platform for Creating Social Websites™". http://www.ning.com/.

ad in the forum.[31] The group continues to see growth at an average of 22 members (median 19) a month, and now has 749 members on its roster. Job posts and event listings are frequent, but there isn't much other conversation.

Austin UPA also started as a Ning site, but it 16
migrated to a WordPress blog and Google Group mailing list in July 2010 after Ning dropped support for free sites.[32] This afforded a unique opportunity for analysis – members who migrated might be more engaged in UPA specifically, as IxDA did not exist when UPA first launched. The Ning site contained 245 members at the point of the migration, of which 121 were also present on the then–444-member IxDA list.[33] For the switch, the original membership was asked to rejoin the new list. 100 users joined within the first few days, 133 joined by the end of the year, and there are 183 total members today, including the same overlap percentage (90 members). Not counting the initial spike, the Google Group sees new members join at an av-

---

31. For the first two years, you had to be a registered member to even view events; now, membership is only required to post and RSVP. Only administrators can post to the mailing list.

32. "Austin UPA Website Launch", *Austin UPA mailing list,* 24 Jul 2010. http://dsn.tc/01c-27.

33. Austin UPA Ning membership roster export dated 13 Jul 2010 and IxDA Austin Ning membership roster export dated 26 Dec 2010.

erage rate of 5 members per month; whether due to the decrease in join rate, increased specialization, or other factors, only one third of new members will end up joining IxDA as well (although members of both are twice as likely to have joined IxDA first).[34] The blog supports comments, but they are rarely made, and log-ins are not shared between the site and the list.

Austin UX started out as a mailing list, blog, and monthly lunch. I don't have participation information on the blog,[35] but at the time the original site was disbanded, the list had 33 members. It now has 99, but the subscribers rarely post; they seem to use it only to receive the weekly list of design-related events. I supplement the mailing list with a Twitter account,[36] which tries to follow as many local design-related people and organizations as possible, and its followers have

---

34. Austin UPA Google Groups membership roster export dated 24 Oct 2011, provided by Craig Tomlin. IxDA Austin Ning membership roster export dated 22 Oct 2011.

35. Unfortunately, the site was hacked shortly before it closed, and I was unable to find a preserved copy. The mailing list archives were kept members-only.

36. "Austin UX", *Twitter.* http://dsn.tc/01c-26.

increased at an average of four per week,[37] despite not directly participating in conversations.[38]

In fact, there appears to be no online, public 18
Austin design community, when either defined as *design-related conversation centered around Austin-based individuals*, or as *conversations within the online presences for the Austin design communities*. I viewed this as a bad thing; it seemed like a substantially unmet need to have no way to sample the pulse of local designers, or to find someone to talk with in person. Shouldn't it be easiest to find like-minded professionals when they're down the proverbial street?

Designers are finding their sense of com- 19
munity elsewhere. As you'll see in the next section, it's not primarily through in-person meetings. Even the 130-odd Austin designers I follow with the AustinUX Twitter account

---

37. From the dates of Twitter follow notification emails from 30 Sep 2010 through 22 Dec 2011, with notable spikes around SXSW and the week of the happy hour from the introduction. Details available on http://distance.cc.

38. I do not run the LinkedIn group of the same name, but almost all of its activity is job postings.

don't seem to talk much amongst themselves;[39] rather, I believe they primarily communicate through location-independent venues such as the parent IxDA list, or through sites like Forrst,[40] Behance,[41] or Dribbble.[42] This idea is supported anecdotally in published interviews with local designers, including creative director Phil Coffman[43] and artist Shyama

39. At any given time, Twitter only exports the last 800 tweets from your timeline. Of 736 tweets written by 136 follows over 4 days, 5:52:12 in the middle of December 2011, exclusive of @AustinUX's own tweets and tweets to @AustinUX, 60 tweets were between 19 followers: 8% of Austin designer tweets were between the 13% of accounts which knew of each other. If you remove tweets between two known couples, that number drops to 47 between 17 accounts, or 6% between 12%. Details available on http://distance.cc.

40. "Forrst is a community for developers and designers". http://forrst.com/.

41. "Behance is the Creative Professional Platform". http://www.behance.net/.

42. "Dribbble is show-and-tell for designers". http://dribbble.com/.

43. "'Is it important to you to be part of a creative community of people?' …I finally made a blog and signed up for Twitter and my eyes were opened… We've been doing Dribbble meet-ups…" "Phil Coffman", *The Great Discontent*, last modified 29 Nov 2011. http://dsn.tc/01c-25.

Timeline of Austin's Local Community

1994

- Pentagram's office opens.

1996

- Frog Design's office opens.

2004

- Frog Design hosts its first SXSW party.

2005

- Razorfish opens its Austin office.

2008

- Adaptive Path opens its Austin office.
- Possible Worldwide opens its Austin office.

JANUARY 2008

- Kyra Edeker hosts an unexpectedly successful happy hour for UX designers at an Austin bar.

SEPTEMBER 2008

- Julie Lowe launches Austin UPA's site.

NOVEMBER 2008

- Tori Breitling launches UX Book Club Austin.
- Austin UX launches and holds its first meeting.

JANUARY 2009

- Austin UPA holds its first meeting.
- UX Book Club Austin holds its first meeting.

FEBRUARY 2009

- Control of IxDA Austin is turned over to Tori Breitling.

March 2009

- IxDA Austin holds its first meeting.

April 2009

- Frog Design hosts an IxDA Austin event.

July 2009

- UX Book Club Austin holds its final meeting.
- Austin UPA migrates from Ning to Google Groups after Ning drops its free support.

January 2010

- Vitorio Miliano begins holding UX workshops patterned after the work of Toastmasters International.

August 2010

- Vitorio Miliano stops holding his regular workshops.
- Austin UX closes.

September 2010

- Austin UX relaunches.

October 2010

- Adaptive Path holds a happy hour.

September 2011

- Frog Design hosts another IxDA Austin event.

Golden,[44,45] both of whom talk about their "creative communities" as being online, rather than local and online, or local and in-person.

Experiences With a New Local Community

My understanding of unmet community needs revolved around criticism and feedback. I wanted to brainstorm, and solicit feedback on designs from more experienced professionals. I sought input from those who could suggest design patterns, best practices, and competitive insights. I wanted to occasionally check in with them to confirm I'm "doing it right", ideally with critiques both during and after the design process. This would give me (and others) a way to both practice design fundamentals and learn how to apply new techniques. This was a persistent need in my own professional development, and in casual conversations with coworkers across different companies and during local meetups, I felt I wasn't the only one.

---

44. "After joining Twitter, Facebook, and Dribbble, a website that allows designers to share their portfolios, Golden noticed people were beginning to take an interest in her work." Jessica Lee, "Shyama Golden uses social media, local venues to show paintings", *Daily Texan*, 13 Sep 2011. http://dsn.tc/01c-23.

45. On reading a draft of this essay, Golden remarked over text message, "Also very much what I experienced in Austin, always thought it was just me." She has since moved to San Francisco.

21 My beliefs were partially reinforced during the design workshops I held in 2010: people always showed up, but I was surprised by their professional diversity. Attendees seemed to average only 50% professional designers: students, developers, and managers comprised the rest. People were interested in a variety of workshop activities – brainstorming, concepting, problem solving, sketching – but they wanted to end each session with a tangible, applied result instead of abstract knowledge. This, along with their irregular attendance,[46] made it difficult to successfully assign "homework" or to support work over multiple workshops.[47] The amount of time and effort necessary to run a workshop (8-16 hours of preparation, 20+ hours to document the results) was a possible reason no one ever volunteered to run one, and only three organizations specifically requested to hold a workshop in support of their ventures.

22 Design-related practice outside of one's work day appears to require interesting, fun, atypical elements and immediately tangible results. Practicing formal critiques or delivering presentations was "too much like work," as one attendee put it. I wondered if current

---

46. Most people would not attend every single week: every other meeting was more common, or at best two or three contiguous meetings.

47. The lone attempt failed due to no overlap in attendees across workshops.

practitioners felt their education and experience provided all the training they needed. Or, maybe they felt their workplaces should encourage any additional training, and if they're not currently doing it, it doesn't need to be done.

Discovering Community Needs

In February 2011, after being prompted by 23
user experience evangelist Sara Summers, I designed a 27-question survey for Austin's design community.[48] It was sent to the IxDA Austin, Austin UPA, Austin UX, and Refresh Austin mailing lists, and it remained open for twelve days, garnering 103 responses.

A little over half of the respondents gave 24
a design-related job title, and up to 86% of respondents worked primarily on the web. Despite the lack of uniform connection to the design industry, there were few statistically

---

48. A copy of the survey as presented to users, as well as its analysis, is available on http://distance.cc.

significant differences between designers and non-designers,[49] suggesting many types of employees, managers, producers, directors, developers, researchers, and freelancers suffer from the same problems.

I asked a mixture of questions I felt would help define the community's makeup, engagement, and experience. To provide a measurement against national figures, some questions were copied verbatim from A List Apart's 2010 web design survey.[50] As ALA found when they launched their survey in 2007, it would seem no one had surveyed local design communities to discover their makeup or their needs. The closest the overarching design community has are "salary and benefits" surveys conducted

49. *Design-related titles* (some written in): Creative, Designer, HCD Lead, Hybrid, Information Architect, Interaction Designer, Interface Designer/UI Designer, UI Developer/UX Designer, Usability Expert/Consultant/Lead, UX Architect, UX Designer/Consultant/Lead, User Researcher, Web Designer, Writer, Editor, Art Director, Creative Director.
Non-design-related titles: Business Analyst, Marketer, Media Coordinator, Product Manager, Web Administrator, Web Director, Web Producer, Web Service Director, Founder, Developer, Senior UI Developer, Software Engineer, and Project Manager.

50. The survey has now closed, but you can see an analysis of its results at ALA Staff, "Findings from the Web Design Survey 2010", *A List Apart*. http://dsn.tc/01c-24.

by UPA,[51] STC,[52] and the IA Institute,[53] which don't look for the same sort of data. Our 103 local responses compare favorably with IAI's 282 for their 2010 national salary survey and their 105 national responses for a "local leaders" survey in 2009,[54] as well as STC Austin's range of "75-150" for their regional salary survey.

Some of the results were expected, such as a 26
strong relationship between where people lived and where they worked, and that weekday evenings were preferred meeting times. Furthering the idea of a distinct event-attending subgroup, 47% reported they don't attend events because they don't have time, and 36% don't keep track of events at all. Write-in comments mentioning family obligations, scheduling conflicts, and transportation issues all lend credence to convenience being a major factor around attendance, but the questionnaire wasn't specific enough to explore this problem more deeply.

The results around the community en- 27
gagement questions were surprising. Of all who responded, 74% regularly collaborate with other designers, suggesting even

---

51. "Salary Surveys", *Usability Professionals Association.* http://dsn.tc/01c-33.
52. "Salary Survey Results Available", *STC Austin.* http://dsn.tc/01c-30.
53. "Salary Survey", *IA Institute.* http://dsn.tc/01c-28.
54. "Local Leaders Survey", *IA Institute.* http://dsn.tc/01c-31.

lone designers (35% of respondents) can find help, but the survey questions weren't able to conclusively say how help was found.

In addition, more than half of respondents reported ten or more years in the field, which seems to be a lot of expertise. Was that a contributing factor to such a large proportion of the community not attending events? It turns out there is a statistically significant difference.[55] Respondents who reported over ten years of experience were more likely to say they had no time to attend events,[56] and were less likely to say they don't keep track,[57] compared to people with fewer than ten years of experience. It is assumed that senior people are more likely to have families and more complicated work schedules, so despite the apparent likelihood that they know what is going on in the community, they do not have enough time to attend. What explains junior- and mid-level practitioners having the time (at least, not reporting that they don't have the time), but not keeping track of events? Is it an issue with the individuals, the organizations, or both?

---

55. Dr. Llewyn Paine, a cognitive psychologist and Austin UPA chapter treasurer, computed the statistical significance for the survey results.

56. $X^2(1, N = 82) = 12.25, p < .001$

57. $X^2(1, N = 82) = 16.86, p < .001$

Regardless of experience, senior respondents were no more or less likely to be interested in the fundamentals of design than anyone else. Most respondents sought basics of IA and UX, brainstorming, sketching, and prototyping; more than half wanted to learn user research, ethnographies, customer development, A/B testing, metrics, and feedback systems. Mentoring, critiques, criticism, and processes led the pack of missing features in the workplace, along with contacting end users, customer research, and market research. Can a mature, well-supported local community really still require education about the basics? 29

A Failure of Perspective

Given the available information, it appears that industry and national organizations have neglected us for years. A few motivated individuals rise above this to spearhead local groups, but they're going it alone. Looking at participation, we don't see any evidence of a public, online, local community, and anecdotes suggest people are finding a sense of community elsewhere. 30

I started a new community, and found that participants want to conduct professional activities without them feeling like work. I conducted a survey, and found that people are collaborating somehow, but the most senior people don't have time to attend events, the 31 most junior people don't know what events are happening, and everyone still wants to learn the basics. How do all of these pieces fit?

They don't. 32

I asked at the outset: does Austin exist between these two perspectives? I believe the answer to be no, because "Austin" as a cohesive design community does not exist at all. Rather, Austin contains a loose collection of dozens, perhaps even hundreds of micro-communities centered around workplaces, with social events being the driver to get people to interact outside of them. 33

What cohesive community could there be without ongoing support? Substantially motivated individuals have been necessary to keep the local organizations going, and they receive little to no support from local companies or parent organizations. Without sustainable talent development, or national or global chapters assisting local chapters with marketing and technology, every group has had ongoing problems with awareness, attendance, adoption, and infrastructure. 34

What kind of community could exist without awareness? At each of eight informal lunches I hosted through IxDA Austin, there were a handful of user experience designers, interaction designers, and user researchers who had never heard of the IxDA, the UPA, or Austin UX: in fact, they attended because someone personally 35 invited them. The same experience persists at IxDA happy hours: they've been practicing interaction design for years, and have interaction designer friends, but have never heard of the IxDA existing either locally or globally. Austin UPA, IxDA Austin, UX Book Club Austin, and Austin UX have all lain fallow in the past, because an organizer wasn't motivated enough.

What kind of community could exist without engagement? There appears to be little Austin-specific online chatter. Experienced designers know what's going on, but they don't have the time for it; and junior designers have the time, but they don't keep up. Everyone yearns for a more supportive work environment, but they want to keep it at work, Mondays through Thursdays. Any free time must be expended on something fun and new; and even then, most people prefer **passive enrichment**: learning from web sites, rather than attending training in person. Unfortunately, the survey wasn't detailed enough to discover how respondents were applying what they learned, if they were truly learning at all; after all, idle time spent on design blogs is very different from active practice.[58] And even if you build a great local community, some people simply won't give up their free time for any reason.

58. "Call Yourself a Practitioner? Prove it", Nathaniel Davis, last modified 9 Jan 2012. http://dsn.tc/01c-29.

Do sociological theory or group theory explain these trends, and offer a way forward? If Austin truly is not a community of practice, can one be made? Should it? If designers aren't getting what they need from their workplaces, can local social organizations support them? 37

Four New Premises

Looking for theoretical solutions, I turned to academic and popular literature: primarily small group research in social psychology,[59] supplemented by related material in other fields like organizational culture, activity theory, and social software design. 38

Writer and researcher Clay Shirky provided an accurate and accessible adaptation of 50 years of sociological research by Bion and others,[60] and social interaction designer Xianhang Zhang offered several compelling anecdotes.[61] Etienne Wagner's *Communities of Practice*[62] was not as helpful as I had hoped, and the harmonious foundations laid out in Peter Block's *Community:* 39

---

59. Also called "group dynamics" by many researchers.

60. "A Group Is Its Own Worst Enemy", Clay Shirky, last modified 1 Jul 2003. http://dsn.tc/01c-32. I cite similar sources elsewhere in this essay.

61. "Social Software Sundays #2 - The Evaporative Cooling Effect," Xianhang Zhang, last modified 10 Oct 2010. http://dsn.tc/01c-36.

62. Etienne Wenger, *Communities of Practice,* Cambridge University Press, 1998.

the Structure of Belonging[63] are unproven. I don't cite research in activity theory or chaordic organizational theory, as I don't think either field is directly relevant at this time.

**Plausible hypothesis 1: Most cities don't 40
harbor local, public design communities.** Rather, there are motivated actors seeking fulfillment in groups and companies which serve their own needs. Marvin E. Shaw says "people join groups in order to satisfy some individual need."[64] These needs can include affiliation (wanting to find someone to commiserate with), or to fulfill needs from outside the group (appearing to learn more to advance at work).

This could also be something of an American 41
problem. In many European countries, the apprenticeship system still exists and is sometimes legally mandated, requiring companies to foster potential future employees and ensure a community is self-sustaining. Here, however, designers – and professionals in all sorts of fields – often go it alone.[65] More than half the respondents in our survey had at least one other designer in their workplace, and while it's possible to find community with as few as

---

63. Peter Block, *Community: the Structure of Belonging*, Berrett-Koehler, 2008.
64. Marvin E. Shaw, *Group Dynamics: The Psychology of Small Group Behavior*, McGraw-Hill, 1976, p. 106.
65. "Being a UX Team of One", Leah Buley, last modified 18 Mar 2009. http://dsn.tc/01c-34.

two other people,[66] small, insular groups don't grow the networks and leadership of larger ones. The demonstrated need for a motivated actor to launch and sustain an organization suggests that, should Tori Breitling falter or the current UPA board fail to sustain interest, Austin would lose its nascent public design scene.

What to do about it? First, given the frac- 42
tured nature of the existing local and global community organizations, are better local communities even needed? Is there value in being a "designer in Austin" versus a "designer at X agency", which just happens to be in Austin, or an "IxDA member" of which the nearest chapter is in Austin? The value of an "Austin design community" should not be assumed.

Second, it should be established what needs 43
the existing communities are filling. Can these needs be filled in more routine ways? In the cases of senior practitioners not having time, and junior practitioners not knowing what's going on, would fixed events improve awareness, if publicized well in advance? STC Austin, for example, establishes and publishes the entire year of its fortnightly lunches at the start of every year. Organizers would then be free to focus on more unique events, making it less traumatic to

---

66. W. R. Bion, *Experiences in Groups*, Basic Books, 1961, p. 26.

the community if an organizer steps down, because the social framework would still persist.[67]

Third, are there ways in which better software can address group paradoxes?[68] As groups formalize their structures to the extent that their members require structure,[69] is there an effective way to organically automate ad-hoc group forming without violating social customs? Shirky echoes Tuckman[70] and other academics in saying that social software developers, not unlike social psychologists, tend to repeat their mistakes by not understanding earlier research, which results in similar theories existing without enough empirical evidence.[71]

---

67. This is because small groups often split their leadership responsibilities across task-based leaders and socio-emotional leaders. See also A. Paul Hare, *Handbook of Small Group Research,* Free Press, 1976, p. 303.

68. For an example of group paradoxes, Shirky describes a party that you're disinterested in – but stay at – until everyone seems to simultaneously want to leave. This is one of many natural group behaviors that software never replicates; in this example, unless you're 4chan, there's always group persistence in group software.

69. Marvin E. Shaw, *Group Dynamics: The Psychology of Small Group Behavior,* McGraw-Hill, 1976, p. 285.

70. Bruce W. Tuckman, "Stages of Small-Group Development Revisited", *Group and Organizational Studies* 2(4): 426, Dec 1977.

71. The design of better group support software is left as an exercise for the reader.

Plausible hypothesis 2: Most designers 45
don't believe in design as a profession. Bion doesn't use the term "participation inequality",[72] but he notes complaints that 80% of patients were "shirkers", comparing this to equivalent problems facing organizations and groups world-wide.[73] Is it truly unexpected to suppose only 20% of your community cares and acts more than the rest? How else to explain the dominant desires for fundamental training, for passive learning, for nearly a third who only do design 9-to-5?

A profession can provide solidarity, spe- 46
cialized training, ethics, and standards. More established professions, like sports, law, and medicine, require ongoing education, training, and reinforcement, and they work to sustainably advance members regardless of where they're

72. The Pareto principle, also known as the 80-20 rule, is an illustration of a power law, where an outsized portion of events – in this case, active participation – are the result of a comparable minority of attributes (here, the number of total possible participants). Participation inequality in online communities is often expressed as the 90-9-1 rule: 90% never contribute, 9% occasionally contribute, and 1% account for an outsize majority of contributions. It's conceivable that real-world communities would follow a similar breakdown if it were possible to track them as accurately. See also "Participation Inequality: Encouraging More Users to Contribute", Jakob Nielsen. http://dsn.tc/01c-35.

73. W. R. Bion, *Experiences in Groups*, Basic Books, 1961, p. 18-19.

employed.[74] Even when a profession requires only certain types of lifelong education, its practioners often find value in additional methods, such as coaching.[75] Design has no such codifications, but the UPA and IxDA were founded in part to provide these elements.[76] Still, the lack of professional standing means designers are not acculturated to believe these things are necessary, nor do they believe they have a personal responsibility to support their field's advancement, resulting in the acceptance of inadequate

---

74. For example, athletes work with coaches and trainers throughout their careers; a medical residency is effectively an apprenticeship which hospitals are required to support; meanwhile, lawyers can pass their state bar exam, and be licensed regardless of their practicing status.

75. Atul Gawande, "Personal Best: Top Athletes and Singers Have Coaches. Should You?" *The New Yorker*, 3 Oct 2011. http://dsn.tc/01c-37.

76. "It's Time We Got Respect", Bruce Tognazzini, last updated 28 Oct 2003. http://dsn.tc/01c-38.

working conditions and the unsustainable practices of not training up junior designers.[77]

What to do about it? Bion and Nielsen independently suggest that disparate engagement levels are a fundamental feature of groups. Furthermore, today's designers don't believe they need ongoing development, and so they don't seek it out. This hurts the local design community because its would-be members see no value in it. Today's designers do not demand work environments more conducive to traditional design practices, with training and critiques and codified processes, so they do not receive them. This hurts the local design community because it lowers the effectiveness and value of all designers throughout the city. If there is any value in a local design community, it may be in declaring principles for designers to follow, improving outreach for and education

77. "I think the number one reason there is a dirth [sic] of mid-level designers is because we (the big we meaning companies, hiring managers, managers) failed to make them. Did we expect them to grow on trees? No. We choose not to create them. We choose not to hire junior people and train them into mid-level designers. We choose to hire only senior designers for various reasons. So the solution is right there - if we want them - we have to commit to designing environments and organizational structures that will support the creation of mid-level designers." Will Evans, comment on Jeff Gothelf, "Why Are There So Few Mid-Level UX Designers?" *The Hired Guns*, 29 Sep 2011. http://dsn.tc/01c-39.

about those values to reduce participation inequality, and collectively pressuring local industries to meet those basic professional needs.

Plausible hypothesis 3: There is not 48
enough high-end value for senior practitioners. Zhang talks about disinterested, high-value members leaving a community, thus setting it on a path to mediocrity. By proxy, could high-value members not join in the first place if the group is already perceived as being mediocre?

Online communities often attempt egali- 49
tarianism, and the IxDA was founded on principles of inclusion and openness. But humans are social, status-seeking animals, and successful, long-term, real-world organizations have "elitist promotion structures". Zhang uses the example of putting high-value contributors on a pedestal as a way of encouraging their continued favor, and participation in his own Product Design Guild[78] is by invitation only. Designers are not immune to special treatment, no matter their experience level.

What to do about it? We infer things in 50
the survey data that may or may not be true. Namely, we assume those with ten years of experience are true senior practitioners. We assume their reasons for not attending are true. We conflate experience with contribution value. Moving forward, it is necessary

---

78. http://productdesignguild.com/.

for each community to determine what it seeks to gain from high-value contributors.

If high-value contribution – whether in the form of knowledge sharing, group leadership, mentoring, standard setting, or other functions – does not come with experience, perhaps the most interesting conversations can be (or are already being) held without the most experienced practitioners. The absence of a demographic does not necessarily mean the community has lost anything. If their presence is desired or needed, then methods for drawing them in can be applied, whether through tailored content or personal invitations. 51

Plausible hypothesis 4: Either there is a shadow design community of private groups, or the Austin community is too immature or fractured to support such a shadow community. Zhang references the "shadow community" of private events and groups in San Francisco as being where "all the real work in the Valley is done", and comments if you are any good and can network, you'll find yourself with an invitation into a small part of it. 52

Caleb Clark's mailing list[79] illustrates the beneficial nature of private communities. As his list grew too large, he shut it down, but he gave key members a new list address, and they 53

---

79. Derek M. Powazek, *Design for Community*, New Riders, 2002, p. 178.

invited their trusted friends, returning cohesion and community. That I find issues and unmet needs in the public design scene may mean it is the mediocre result of all the high-value contributors being elsewhere. It could also mean for a shadow community to exist, there must be a certain amount of public cohesion which San Francisco exhibits, but Austin does not.

54 *What to do about it?* I am told New York City's design scene started out privately – drinking wine in someone's condo – and later grew into something public, so apparently it can work multiple ways. If the situation is the former, I am not sure anything should be done about it: barriers to entry are necessary for groups to protect themselves. If the situation is the latter, can the tail wag the dog? Would forming an exclusive, private design meeting in Austin push the public, accessible groups to be more competitive?

Local Communities By Design

55 The issues faced by the Austin design community might be shared in other cities, as well as by other types of communities. I imagine New York and San Francisco to have such a density of designers as to be culturally different from any other cities in the country – perhaps the world. If you don't live in New York or San Francisco, then these issues – awareness, attendance, adoption, infrastructure – are likely yours, too. You don't know how

many designers exist, what they do in their jobs, how supportive their workplaces are, what their needs are, what their interests are, and if they talk with other designers. You may only ever see the motivated 20%, 10%, or 1%.

We are an industry that claims to promote 56
measured, analytical design, but we're ignorant of the history of social group design[80] and we're ignorant of the makeup of our own local communities. How can we design a community of practice if we don't study ourselves as users?

Last year's survey was a good start, but bet- 57
ter data could be collected, and as groups make changes to address these issues, ongoing testing and validation is necessary. We've developed a revised survey for 2012, which tries to discover how engaged and experienced your group members are. We've also designed feedback forms for continuous analysis of your progress with each event you hold. In conjunction with this essay, we're making everything available for you to use with your local community group.[81]

---

80. Formed months after Shirky's talk, IxDA violates all of his recommendations for good social group design. It supports none of "handles the user can invest in", "some way in which good works get recognized", "barriers to participation", nor "a way to spare the group from scale" from "A Group Is Its Own Worst Enemy".

81. Dr. Llewyn Paine consulted on the 2012 survey and event response card.

The survey is available online through 58
Qualtrics, a survey tool used especially for qualitative research, and their free trial accounts support up to 250 responses, which should be enough if your response rate is at all comparable to ours from 2011. We provide full documentation on how to release the survey in a section about this essay on the *Distance* website, http://distance.cc. After we analyze the 2012 Austin results, we'll update it with instructions on how you can do the same.

The event response cards are for handing 59
out and collecting at every meeting you hold. They've been designed to match the survey, and along with taking a headcount, they try to tell you how well your event was received, how well it met people's expectations, if the attendees were new or existing members, and their level of engagement. A Google Docs Spreadsheet is provided with a form to make entering responses as easy as possible, with formulas included to display an analysis of the results, automatically. Full instructions are available on http://distance.cc.

For the first time, local leaders have data to 60
compare group growth, sentiment and ongoing practices against. If you're a local leader, give the survey to your community and use the feedback forms in your meetings. If you're not, share this information with your group's organizers and help them adopt the survey and feedback forms. Fight to spread the word and

collect responses. Demand answers from attendees at every event: whether a happy hour or a private lecture. Look at the data and compare it to both the national figures and those from other cities of similar size. We've provided all of our data and recommendations for Austin on http://distance.cc, and we'll be providing additional analysis after publication, including how we've changed. Learn what your community is doing and what it wants. Tell others what you want to see from it. Use this information to help build the community you wish you had.

If you believe in design as a profession, as a community of practice existing in your city, this is the next step. The national organizations can't help you[82] and your industry doesn't support you. Building a thriving local community is up to you.

82. While IxDA compares to AIGA in size with over 20,000 "members," their 2010 report was a tweet: http://dsn.tc/01c-40. In contrast, every AIGA chapter produces an annual report on its membership. STC is the next largest, with a third of the members, and appears to be second to AIGA in formality, surveying for possible improvements at the international level. UPA provides a handbook for chapter leaders, but they have a tenth of the membership. The IA Institute has only a twentieth of the membership. No organizations appear to provide ongoing support for managing local chapters nor discovering local community needs. I discuss the concept of a better company of designers as an outline for a new sort of professional organization in another essay: http://vi.to/better/.

About the authors

Nick Disabato helps other people make *Distance.* An interaction designer by trade, he cares about the way that we talk with each other, and wants to make our conversations more constructive meaningful. He can usually be found on his bike somewhere in Chicago.

Ben Jackson is a writer and app developer living in Brooklyn, New York. He likes clean typography, dirty language, strong coffee, apple pie, and comfortable chairs, and he writes about his obsessions at http://90wpm.com.

Jon Whipple is a designer in Vancouver. He doesn't like to talk about himself in the third person. He likes to work. He is a Professional Member of the Society of Graphic Designers of Canada.

Vitorio Miliano is a designer in Austin, TX. He likes talking about genuine outbreaks of the future and thinks a lot about design mentoring, community and education. His personal work includes preserving and digitizing public domain works, Bildungsroman and subversive children's literature, ambient information, ubiquitous computing and ambient intelligence, digital/physical crossover devices, and experimental hardware.

Write for DISTANCE

Distance is an attempt to create a good place for both readers *and* writers, and it wouldn't be anything without the contributions of others. **This means you.** We have a track record of publishing well-edited, researched essays that ask the big *why* questions about our field.

Most of *Distance*'s authors have written for us after reading an issue, and so far, every single author of a *Distance* essay has expressed interest in writing more frequently. Writing for us gives people the momentum and confidence to keep at it; towards that end, we love working with people who don't have long track records of successful writing

If you have a great idea, we can make something fantastic together. Please don't hesitate to email us at we@distance.cc; we'll start small, bat ideas around, and turn it into something great.

For more information on our editorial process, head over to http://distance.cc/write/.

✤

MailChimp

Colophon

Text and footnotes are set in Documenta, made by Frank E. Blokland and distributed through Dutch Type Library. Headers and page numbers are set in Flama by Mário Feliciano. Fleurons are from Fell Flowers by Igino Marini. Greek text is Neohellenic, designed by Victor Scholderer and digitized by the Greek Font Society.

All errata are at http://distance.cc/errata/. While all cited links were active at the time of publication, if you find a dead URL that's not listed on the errata page, please get in touch.

Distance is proudly made in Chicago.

ISBN 978-0-9850515-0-1

Get in touch:
http://distance.cc
we@distance.cc

US $20.00

9 780985 051501 >

DISTANCE 02

concerns *extracurriculars.*

Wherein:

Cassie McDaniel asserts that we can change the world more easily when we're embedded in foreign situations.

Sharlene King wants us to create homework for ourselves, so we can improve our own skills.

Francisco Inchauste proposes a way to restore meaning and significance to what and how we build.

✤

DISTANCE's essays don't exist in a vacuum. We encourage you to excerpt and discuss these essays with others. You have free reign to quote as much as you need to get your point across. Good writing begins conversations, and we're listening. Visit *Distance*'s website at http://distance.cc to read and remark on others' responses.

If you have any questions, email us at we@distance.cc and we'll make it right.

Publisher's thoughts

by **Nick Disabato**

nickd@nickd.org, @nickd

Nary a month after our first issue's launch party, our second issue is in the can. I'm extremely proud of our authors and their essays, and I'm honored and humbled that you have chosen to stay with us.

I have two goals with *Distance*: to elevate the quality of conversation about our field, and to expose unheard, talented people to a wider audience. I know that neither goal is terribly novel or interesting, but they're increasingly difficult to achieve. I'm patient enough to know that it may take a long time before we start to see any meaningful change. In the meantime, I love helping others make each issue that we put out the door.

Our first issue was a grab bag: each essay had a different subject area, critical angle, and research direction. This is my first attempt at refining and focusing a conversation around a specific goal. As I line up authors for each future issue of *Distance*, whomever signs on first will be able to determine the issue's theme—which, in turn, will affect the other two essays. Themes are broad so an author's goal can stay open-ended, though:

interesting ideas may come from far-flung places, resisting immediate connection and inference.

As you might have guessed from the front cover, *Distance* 02 is about **extracurriculars**. What do we do outside our day-to-day work? How does our work environment affect us? And how can our work be meaningfully received by our audiences? We offer one way forward for each of these questions, and we seek your input.

Our website, at http://distance.cc, provides a handful of ways you can join the conversation—but the easiest is on your own turf. Post about our essays on your blog. Tweet your initial thoughts @distance. Send us an email, at we@distance.cc, about what you think. Rip our work apart; make it better.

Thanks again for reading, and for all of your ongoing support. Hope you're well.

Take care,
Nick Disabato
May 30, 2012

Authors' thanks

Cassie McDaniel: An enormous thank you to my husband, Mark Staplehurst (aka @britburger), for putting up with months of late nights and stolen weekends while I worked on this essay. Not only did he consistently break one of our rules by cooking for me *and* doing the dishes, he also helped me un-muddle my expressions, offering suggestions and improvements to the writing when they were most needed. Thanks as well to Nancy Kay Clark, editor of Design Edge Canada; and to the writers group at High Park Library in Toronto, who helped me focus the essay and spurred me on toward the finish line with nice things things to say (even if they weren't true).

Sharlene King would like to thank the Chicago Public Library for their incredibly low late fees, extenuating patience, and proximity to work; Nicole, my partner, who in spite of her unending disinterest in design has found me interesting and tolerable; Nick Disabato, for his perpetual state of concern and generosity; and the entire Chicago design community—you know who you are, you pretty young things.

Francisco Inchauste would like to thank the kind editor of this wondrous publication, Nick Disabato, for asking me to be a part of this special thing. Through this essay, I was able to synthesize a perspective on the kind of design I believe in, and hope more of us can practice it in the future. I appreciate some early feedback from Rian van der Merwe that helped to hone the premise. Thank you, reader, because this idea will only come to life through your interpretation, dissidence, and proselytizing. I'm indebted to the writings of Umair Haque for providing great insight into how we can measure meaningful things. I'd also like to thank my wife, Megan, and our amazing kids for showing me what a meaningful life is all about.

Note on citations

Distance exists in quite a few forms: book, PDF, ePub, and Kindle. We know that people read all sorts of ways, and we want the text to fit your reading habits, not the other way around. 1

Most citation methods refer to a work's page number, but only two of *Distance*'s forms have discrete pages. Consistent, understandable citation by page number is impossible, so wayfinding must exist within the actual text. 2

In an attempt to solve this problem, *Distance* doesn't have page numbers. Instead, each essay's paragraph has a little number to the right, as seen here. *These numbers will always be consistent among each format of an issue of* Distance. 3

This is similar to the convention of "purple numbers" in blogging,[1] and it will remove any ambiguity about what's being referenced. As a rule of thumb, where a page number would go, use the **paragraph number** instead. 4

For example, MLA citation should look like Whipple, Jon. "What Designers Know." *Distance* 01: 14–17 for the 14th through 17th paragraphs of Jon Whipple's essay in our first issue. 5

1. See also CIM Community, "Purple Numbers", http://dsn.tc/01x-01 and Simon Willison, "PLinks", http://dsn.tc/01x-02.

I sense a new attitude of buckling down to change entire organizations, to increase public and governmental awareness of the importance of our work, and to seek out opportunities to affect the lives of millions.

—Cennydd Bowles, *A Changing Tide*, at http://dsn.tc/02x-02

The multiplexed multiplicity of personality and identity drives us deeper into the self to search for what cannot be reproduced, devalued, commodified, into the world of intentions, subjective states, secrets. We flock to the aura of the artwork and to the Platonic self: an unmediated self of inimitable, irreducible, meaningful purity. We vigilantly test for forgeries and phonies.

We want what the camera cannot show: a person's fidelity to his innate truth. We want the soul we doubt, the core we have learned isn't there. We want the antidote to personality, the desperate and neurotic fictions of the performative self. We want the inner, abiding fact: may it abide beyond death.

—Mills Baker, *Authenticity and the Deformation of Character*, at http://dsn.tc/02x-01

The Embedded Designer

Changing the world in far-flung industries.

by **Cassie McDaniel**

knockknock@cassiemcdaniel.com, @cassiemc

WHEN I FINISHED SCHOOL, I decided not 1
to find a job right away. Instead, I sold almost everything I owned, stuffed what remained into two bulging suitcases, and bought a one-way ticket to London. Some people told me I was brave (*You've never been to Europe?*); others told me not to go (*It isn't safe for Americans*). I ignored everyone: I was too excited about curry houses on every street corner to worry about visas, exchange rates, or foreign prisons.

In my first couple of months there, I learned 2
the street names fairly quickly, but I never really knew where I was. I was terrified of the surge of rush-hour commuters on the Underground. I wore an unruly orange blouse in a sea of blacks and greys. I recognized accents I nevertheless couldn't understand. Over time, I adjusted. Trash became rubbish, America became the States, statements became questions, and Jay-Z became Jay-Zed. I came to appreciate how London's meandering sprawl reveals a long and layered history—even if wayfinding proved impossible.

A year later, I stood in Waterloo station as 3
hoards of people rushed by to catch their trains. I looked up at the fifty-foot–tall ceilings, the four-faced clock, the vaulted glass roof, the black soot on meticulously engraved walls, and I realized: I had begun to take these things for granted. I had unconsciously acclimated to an entirely new environment, and now I became aware of a monumental internal shift. I recalled my first glimpse of London from the airplane window—the jumble of matchbox flats and the olive-green Thames snaking its way through the chaos—and realized how far I was from everything I used to know, how different I would seem to people who knew me back home.

This Waterloo moment allowed me 4
to reconcile the tough parts about living abroad with the payoff of personal growth. I realized I could adapt to a new environment simply by being immersed in its culture.

Design needs its own Waterloo moment. 5
To get there, we designers need to look to unfamiliar problems in new territories, especially within other industries. In doing this we will find that thoughtful design can be applied everywhere—a simple idea that holds an endless potential for us to not only grow as designers, but to change the world.

Working inside-out

Scott Thomas saw the potential for disruption 6
when he was offered a position at Barack Obama's '08 campaign headquarters.[1] It only took a day for Thomas to accept the offer and trade in his freelance life for a full-time gig.

Over the following year, Thomas built a 7
team capable of designing on the fly in response to immediate campaign needs. It was critical to embed the team directly into the campaign, rather than to hire freelancers, because insight into the culture for which they were designing proved a valuable asset. For example, if Thomas had been asked to implement a stack of posters or stickers, such a predetermined solution would have limited the design possibilities that allowed greater insight and cohesion within the whole campaign.

Closed briefs, such as designing posters 8
or stickers, menus, websites, or book covers, result in simple assets. These projects are often easy and profitable; they are simple to cost out and familiar to execute. Alternatively, open briefs, which call for designers to completely reimagine how people interact with our clients,

---

1. "To ensure the impeccable execution so prized by [Sol] Sender when he created the 'O' logo, the campaign began to realize that in-house designers were needed to manage the creation and production of future materials". Scott Thomas, *Designing Obama,* Post Press, 2010, p. 33. http://dsn.tc/02a-05.

are few and far between and are usually considered too ambitious for existing budgets.

Yet closed briefs often indicate a missed op- 9
portunity to source the true root of a design problem, which squanders design's potential. That is the key message behind design thinking, or a hands-on design methodology as a means to innovation. However, no amount of design thinking will seamlessly integrate design into complex systems without deep, long-term commitment on our part—and that can't happen through freelance work or short-term agency projects. We can really only thoroughly understand a problem if we're positioned closer to our end users or embedded in their culture.[2]

Would Thomas have been able to redefine 10
political campaign design if his work was dictated by a traditional client relationship? Would his work have fit the campaign's shifting context if he was briefed on what to create, rather than assessing for himself what was needed? I doubt his work would have had as much integrity or as long-lasting an effect.

---

2. Heather Loftiss tackles the pros and cons of in-house design teams versus running one's own agency in her *AIGA* article, "Jumping In from the Outside", 27 Feb 2012. http://dsn.tc/02a-02.

Design's innate adaptability

Tim Brown, IDEO's CEO and president, 11
sorts the creative process into three phases: inspiration, ideation, and implementation.[3] During the inspiration phase, we gather resources and insights through creative briefs, personas, competitive landscapes, asking questions, and listening to what clients both do and don't say. This process, says Brown, is available to everyone: engineers, businesspeople, and entrepreneurs.[4]

While design processes are available to 12
anyone, regular experience with the creative process makes the designer particularly adaptable to new environments. An eagerness to understand the nature of our design challenges is part of our mandate. We ask tough questions of our clients and their industries. We need to know: Why are things done this way? What problem is it solving? What can we get rid of to make this simpler? Designers are receptive to new input

---

3. Tim Brown, *Change By Design: How Design Thinking Transforms Organizations and Inspires Innovation*, HarperCollins Business, 2009.

4. Design needs constraint to function well. The more information we have, the more constraint we have, and constraint forces creative solutions to the surface.

by definition, and that makes us inherently more malleable than other kinds of workers.[5]

This adaptability means designers are not only adept at facing change, but also at initiating it. Andy Epstein, in-house designer evangelist at AIGA New York and author of *The Corporate Creative*, agrees, saying:[6]

> As a group, designers possess a powerful set of talents, beliefs and aptitudes that are often lacking in today's average corporate culture, but that are uniquely suited to effecting change for more responsible, humane, and sustainable business practices.

In short, designers crave change. We want new inspirations, we get tired of the same old challenges, and we're willing to make sacrifices in order to have an inspiring and challenging environment. Scott Thomas is just one example —he was ready to take on the Obama campaign without any experience in politics. This type of enthusiasm isn't unusual for designers.

---

5. Adaptability is built even deeper into the design process, where critique is a foundational skill. Web designers, too, are a breed of their own; quickly-evolving technologies mandate the need to stay current.
6. Andy Epstein, "Design for Change: An Inside Job", *AIGA*, 21 Apr 2011. http://dsn.tc/02a-04.

A better way of working: big wheel, little wheel

Today's global challenges—such as poverty, 14
education, the environment, human rights, and health epidemics—are extremely complex and won't be solved by a single person working in isolation. When many players must work together, the **hub and spoke model**, which requires several independent arms to join up in a central hub to exchange ideas or services, is a common method of organization. This model makes sense at the management level.[7] For example, airlines route passengers through a handful of centralized airports so they can more easily manage travel schedules and maintain profits. But the model also has gross inefficiencies that can be bad for individuals. Airline schedules, for example, have peak travel times where demand is predictably higher than par, which can create unnecessary congestion and domino delays for travelers.

Interdisciplinary collaboration sometimes 15
provides similar frustrations, despite a team's best intentions. For example, clients may ask one agency to develop their brand, another to come up with digital strategy, another to create a website, and yet another to develop

---

7. The *hub and spoke model* is traditionally used to describe aviation or distribution paths where several routes pass through one central location to maximize efficiency and, sometimes, profit. See also http://dsn.tc/02a-03.

the website—but it can be difficult for so many large teams to communicate with each other. One of the best ways to counteract the inefficiencies of the hub and spoke model is to internalize a team of experts, structured as many smaller wheels as opposed to one large wheel.

16 Many smaller wheels means more opportunities for exchange between players, which includes exposure to new and different ideas, new sources of inspiration, more opportunities to open up and share the creative process, to build trust, to enable individuals, and to respond to immediate needs. In short, people collaborate more easily in smaller groups. But for this to be effective, we designers need to be willing to cooperate with other industries.

Disrupting insularity

17 Language shows how exclusive industries can be. Within any discipline is a unique vocabulary that outsiders struggle to understand. Design uses acronyms like IA, PDF, NDA, FPO, COB, and SoW, for example, that carry different meanings depending on their context. The same, of course, exists within other industries. Insular language typically discourages collaboration. It poses a learning curve, for instance, and unless we force ourselves to admit ignorance and ask questions in the moment, it can be a barrier to meaningful collaboration. Quirks like these are ripe for disruption.

The internet is a tool routinely used to disrupt traditional industries. Airbnb disrupted the travel accommodation industry by allowing individuals to viably compete with hotels.[8] Publishing companies have revolutionized their revenue models by accepting ebooks and paywalls as major sources of income.[9] Educational institutions post their courses online for free; musicians put their discographies on Bandcamp[10] and SoundCloud.[11] Disruptions share a few key traits:[12] 18

- the open flow of ideas;
- the sharing of resources;
- the empowerment of the individual;
- and a sudden shift of revenue away from established players.

---

8. Alex Cocotas, "Airbnb's Revenue Explodes", *Business Insider*, 13 Mar 2012. http://dsn.tc/02a-01.
9. Steve Ladurantaye, "Publishers Take Heart from NYT Paywall Success", *The Globe and Mail*, 20 Mar 2012. http://dsn.tc/02a-18.
10. http://bandcamp.com.
11. http://soundcloud.com.
12. Horace Dediu, "What is Disruption and How Can it be Harnessed?", *Asymco*, 12 Mar 2012. http://dsn.tc/02a-13.

Startups have led this charge, and they often 19
embrace designers as founding members[13]—but what if a designer doesn't want to be an entrepreneur, and what if they don't want to work in an agency? Where will they find their place? Fortunately, the opportunities for design are much more extensive than what is currently most visible. Embed a designer into other social settings, and we can make valuable contributions to these disciplines—as well as garner a better understanding of our own creative process. Imagine if we took another look at the way the world farms, pursues justice, teaches kids, or empowers communities.

When art stopped being science

While a hundred years ago working with 20
people in unrelated fields would have seemed absurd, five hundred years ago the crossover between art and design and our scientific counterparts was far from novel. Historically, most noteworthy scholars were accomplished in multiple subject areas including art and science.[14] Leonardo da Vinci's anatomical drawings, for example, were equally informed by scientific

---

13. Laurie Seagall, "Silicon Valley is Desperate for Designers", *CNN Money*, 6 Apr 2012. http://dsn.tc/02a-14.

14. Rihll argues that most, as opposed to many, early scholars and academics were skilled polymaths. C.J. Tuplin and T.E. Rihll (eds.), *Science and Mathematics in Ancient Greek Culture*, Oxford University Press, 2002.

methods as they were by concepts of balance, proportion, stroke, and chiaroscuro. Ancient scholars Zhang Heng from China[15] and Imhotep from Egypt[16] were polymaths. Being well-rounded was integral to education from very early on throughout the world, well before the European Renaissance. Multi-talented scholars not only pioneered engineering, architecture, medicine, and mathematics, but they also shaped art, music, philosophy and literature.

The term "scientist" didn't even exist until 150 years ago, having first surfaced in a proposal by William Whewell, an English polymath, in the mid 1800s.[17] In the late 1800s, Great Britain established a governmental body called the Science and Art Department, a consolidation of several institutions concerned with practical disciplines—art, design, and both hard and soft sciences; and at the time, miners and geologists sat comfortably alongside artists and

15. Zhang Heng invented the world's first seismograph to measure earthquakes and was an accomplished astronomer and poet. Yeong-chung E. Lien, *Zhang Heng, Eastern Han Polymath, His Life and Works* (PhD dissertation), University of Washington, 2011. http://dsn.tc/02a-15.

16. Imhotep is considered to be the first architect of the step pyramids and an early physician. See also "Imhotep", *Encyclopedia Britannica.* http://dsn.tc/02a-17.

17. William Whewell, *The Philosophy of the Inductive Sciences, Volume 2*, Harrison and Co., 1840, p. 416.

designers under the same council.[18] Design was unquestionably labelled a practical art, and design and science were close allies.

Before Whewell's proposal, students 22
acquired skills that naturally overlapped disciplines in order to receive what was considered a well-rounded education. Whewell's introduction of the word *scientist* suggests a distinct beginning for the separation of design and art. Recently, the gap between the arts and the sciences has narrowed enough that we may be able to return to our interdisciplinary roots. Given this, we will have a shot at solving some of the world's tough problems that need creative thinking.

Disappearing barriers

Education is dissolving the barriers between 23
industries, making it easier for us to branch out. There is more shared, democratic knowledge today than ever before, and many companies are taking advantage of unrestricted access to education and resources. University of the People was founded in 2009 as a 100% tuition-free

18. Henry Barnard (ed.), "Science and Art Department and the South Kensington Museum", *The American Journal of Education* 22: 49–50, 1871.

institute for higher-education,[19] while Khan Academy and MIT's OpenCourseWare provide free, in-depth coursework on a diverse range of subjects. Codecademy[20] and Method of Action[21] provide intuitive, flexible formats for learning to program and design. And more platforms keep launching: Pathwright, released in April 2012 by Duo Interactive, allows anyone to create and sell online courses.[22] Never before have we been so well-equipped to accomplish whatever we set our minds to. As another Renaissance polymath, Leon Battista Alberti, once said: "A man can do all things if he will."

Despite the abundance of opportunity, de- 24
signers tend to be relegated (and relegate themselves) to a few niche fields. About.com (perhaps not the preeminent indicator of design trends, but still a top Google result) sorts graphic design graduates into five possible career tracks: advertising, web design, book design, illustration,

---

19. Khan Academy, http://www.khanacademy.org, Massachusetts Institute of Technology, http://ocw.mit.edu, and University of the People, http://www.uopeople.org represent a changing attitude in academia toward free education. Further programs and resources are profiled in Wendy Boswell's article, "Technophilia: Get a Free College Education Online", *Lifehacker*, 25 Sep 2006. http://dsn.tc/02a-16.

20. http://www.codecademy.com.

21. http://method.ac.

22. http://www.pathwright.com.

and branding.[23] These are skills, not careers, yet they are the most familiar paths; marketing and advertising agencies lure graduates with higher salaries and the promise of working with world-renowned brands. But some professionals are starting to ask another question: Is it important work? Cameron Koczon searches for our purpose in his rousing article "An Important Time for Design":[24]

> [The startup world is] ready to believe that design is going to change the world—all we have to do is show that it can. If we succeed, we change the way design is perceived and valued forever. If we fail, design will lose its luster and misguided ideas about what design is may prevail.

As the barriers between fields break down, we should keep trying to answer what design is. Mark MacKay, an interaction designer and co-creator of Method of Action, insightfully describes the differences between art, design, and engineering:[25]

---

23. Eric Miller, "Graphic Design Career Paths", About.com. http://dsn.tc/02a-12.
24. Cameron Koczon, "An Important Time for Design", *A List Apart*, 17 Jan 2012. http://dsn.tc/02a-11.
25. Mark MacKay, "You're Already a Pretty Good Designer", *Method of Action*, 27 Jul 2011. http://dsn.tc/02a-07.

> People often make of design some sort [of] commercial spawn of art. It is not. Design is a discipline in itself, related to engineering, that uses some of art's syntax. It is different from engineering in the sense that engineering looks after the efficiency and robustness the product [sic], and design looks at the interaction between the product and a human being.

Both MacKay and Koczon attempt to define design as it currently exists, but they also exude an idealism about what design is capable of across industries. Although MacKay points out some differences between design and other fields, he also hints that even disparate industries have more in common than might appear at first glance: a shared purpose of building for people.

Designers who seek to cross disciplines 25
have an awful lot of wind in their sails. The big barriers—access, exposure, and inflexible ideologies—seem to have already broken down.

Other industries' good ideas

People often borrow concepts from sister 26
disciplines to advance their own. In the late seventies, architect Christopher Alexander came up with the idea of **design patterns**,[26] or

26. Christopher Alexander's book, *A Pattern Language: Towns, Buildings, Construction,* was written with Sara Ishikawa, Murray Silverstein, Max Jacobson, Ingrid Fiksdahl-King, and Shlomo Angel in 1977, and remains a seminal book on architecture and urban design.

reusable solutions to a common problem. For example, a hospital waiting room and a bus stop are both places in which people wait, so they might share similar environmental needs.

In 1995, Erich Gamma, Richard Helm, Ralph 27
Johnson, and John Vlissides applied design patterns to software, making difficult programming solutions replicable and streamlined.[27] More recently in 2010, Ethan Marcotte borrowed from architecture when he proposed responsive web design, in which designers and developers account for an ever-expanding variety of screen sizes, resolutions, and interaction models. He was inspired by "responsive architecture," where environments physically "bend, flex, and expand as crowds approach them".[28] Without an interest in other disciplines—and without access to their knowledge—programming and web design would look very different today.

A case study: design in healthcare

While these suggestions may sound theoretical, 28
they come from firsthand experience. Healthcare is one of the biggest industries in need of a shake-up, so it is with that in mind that I accepted a job last fall as the first

27. Erich Gamma, et al., *Design Patterns: Elements of Reusable Object-Oriented Software*, Addison-Wesley, 1994.
28. Ethan Marcotte, "Responsive Web Design", *A List Apart*, 25 May 2010. http://dsn.tc/02a-10.

visual designer at Toronto General Hospital's Centre for Global eHealth Innovation.

It is somewhat of a paradox to me that an 29
industry with so much financial backing and so many smart, passionate people can have such low design standards. On first blush, it may be because healthcare practitioners are too busy focusing on much bigger problems. Medical errors contribute to a staggering number of deaths each year,[29] and chronic disease management, preventative medicine, and patient-doctor communication are massive problems for which there are no silver bullets.

Our Centre has an enormous scope of in- 30
novative projects. We evaluate medical devices, examine processes, and assess environments; we design and implement solutions to the problems we find. The team consists of clinical engineers, programmers, nutritionists, hardware engineers, managers, human factors analysts, an industrial designer, and user interface designers. We work closely with our clients and partners, including both internal and

---

29. Rachel Giese reports in "The Errors of Their Ways" published in *The Walrus* Apr 2012 issue that the number of deaths from medical mistakes this year in Canada alone will reach around 24,000. Earlier reports (P. Aspden, et al., *Preventing Medication Errors,* Quality Chasm Series, National Academies Press, 2007) suggest 1.5 million patients are harmed each year in the States because of medication errors, costing hospitals an extra $3.5 billion.

external vendors, but my work usually brings me closest to my colleagues in human factors.

With roots in cognitive psychology, human 31
factors analysts take into account the environmental, cognitive, physical, and organizational considerations for how humans interact with objects, services, or technologies.[30] Donald Norman helped popularize the discipline in *The Design of Everyday Things*,[31] but the field first gained prominence during World Wars I and II to improve pilots' aviation safety. In later years, human factors expanded to high-risk systems like nuclear facilities, where the consequences of error can be catastrophic. When we pinpoint critical safety issues in our devices, we pay attention to what kinds of interactions lead to the most effective change in behavior, as well as to the broader challenge of incorporating good human-centered design into real-world environments.

Over the past few months, I've noticed the 32
vivid contrast between sterile, whitewashed clinical practice and a chaotic, messy designer's environment—although each is desirable in its own way. A new colleague of mine recently described his experience teaching human factors

30. Kim Vicente, *The Human Factor: Revolutionizing the Way We Live with Technology*, Vintage Canada, 2004, pp. 1–4.

31. Donald Norman, *The Design of Everyday Things*, Basic Books, 1988.

engineering at a local design school: "Everything is so messy and unstructured. The students aren't used to grades. Anything goes," he told me. I noted how wonderful that environment sounded, but his discomfort was obvious. This neatly sums up the split: he prefers deadlines, structure, and hierarchy, because those elements have been strong factors throughout his career.

Creative people are often ad-hoc, spontane- 33
ous, and frequently digital-native, but hospitals are structured, well-documented, and often paper-driven. While designers strive to engage and inspire, a healthcare provider strives for their patient's return to normalcy, and while I tend toward creative risk-taking, the consequences can be life-threatening in healthcare. Unconventional interfaces, for example, that prove difficult for nurses to use in high-stress, time-sensitive situations can prevent the necessary delivery of care for patients.

Since joining healthcare, I've had to design in 34
new ways, often finding I share an unexpected commonality with human factors. Both human factors and design employ a similar process for evaluation, for example: what human factors calls a heuristic evaluation,[32] we call a critique. Both design critiques and heuristic evaluations work best when they are specific, focused,

32. Jakob Nielsen's "Ten Usability Heuristics" (2005) outlines guiding principles for achieving successful user interface design. http://dsn.tc/02a-08.

constructive, and tied to objectives; and both draw on intuition during assessment. Both disciplines are also concerned primarily with the user.

But the broad similarities end there. Human 35
factors analysis employs more precise terminology than design: for example, what might be "this isn't quite right" in a design critique would unequivocally be labeled an error in a heuristic evaluation. Designers assess an overall emotional experience, while human factors analysts look for unambiguous, measurable success. Designers also seem to practice greater tolerance for trial and error—and subsequently more failures—when solving a problem. Ultimately, however, we share the same prerogative to make systems better, easier, and safer.

Exposure to new methodologies is chal- 36
lenging the way I work. If colleagues ask the purpose of a mood board, I must examine and validate why a mood board will be useful to the team. This doesn't make me inefficient, though: rather, it forces me to be realistic about design's strengths and weaknesses that I currently take for granted. On the same hand, seeing the ways my colleagues ask participants non-leading questions during usability studies has forced me to examine my own partiality toward certain design feedback. I now strive toward a more unbiased, user-oriented perspective.

My own experience serves as a case study 37
for the kinds of challenges other embedded designers might face. While your daily tasks, preferred work environments, and processes may differ, the opportunity to extend design to other industries is vast and exciting.

The challenges facing embedded designers

Embedding design into other disciplines isn't 38
easy. Good creative environments are difficult to translate to other industries, and designers typically don't want to relinquish their office's perks and culture. Material benefits, however, only serve as motivation for so long. If we address some of the potential discomforts of the embedded designer, we can pull designers into unfamiliar territories, break down the preconceptions of new collaborators, and face the shortcomings of our current design practices.

Physical space

The environment in which we work can have 39
a big influence on first impressions of new industries. Moving from open floor plans to cubicle rows, for example, is a dramatic shift. Office spaces, however, are usually non-negotiable, so how can we encourage better integration into new spaces without too much alteration or expense? One easy way is to make full use of common areas, like a shared lunch space or breakout room, to allow face time between colleagues. These spaces

should provide some impetus for use, like common tools or resources, coffee machines or refrigerators. Pockets of shared physical spaces that encourage interaction will allow different types of workers to coexist.

Creative monopoly

Although design often monopolizes the 40
word "creative" (the "creative department", for instance), there is a staggering amount of creativity in other disciplines, such as in programming and the social sciences. It de-motivates others when we monopolize the word "creative". It is important that colleagues be treated as a unified team, with creativity encouraged among everyone.

Perceived value

At the beginning of 2012, Mike Monteiro 41
shared some resolutions for us in *.net Magazine*, suggesting we branch out from creating glossy veneers or selling things, to social problems like the economy, education, and sustainable food sources:[33]

> We have more processing power, affordable tools, and combined intelligence right this very minute than at any point in the history of design. We are using it to

---

33. Mike Monteiro, "10 New Year's Resolutions for Designers", *.net Magazine*, 3 Jan 2012. http://dsn.tc/02a-09.

build shit. It's time to aim higher. Let's find problems to solve that actually improve people's lives.

As Monteiro suggests, design has become a 42
scene that celebrates itself. By working in fields whose primary enterprise is in sales and marketing, designers reinforce the notion that design has a narrow scope. We need a wake-up call to establish our legitimacy among other industries, and we can begin to dislodge outdated perceptions of design by moving into new contexts.

"If you weren't a designer, what would you have done?"

In a series of interviews in *Bracket*'s first volume, 43
some design industry role models were asked what they might be if not designers. Frank Chimero said he'd be an astronaut; Jessica Hische said she'd work in forensics; Geoff McFetridge said he would have been a professional downhill skier. Other answers ran the gamut: marine biologist, anthropologist, sociologist, writer, ping-pong player, vicar.[34] As designers, the truth is that we have the ability to explore all of these areas while we maintain our day jobs.

---

34. *Bracket* 01 (Anonymous, Sep 2010), http://dsn.tc/02a-06. More answers included a treasure hunter, race car driver, sign painter in Mexico, chef, visual artist, musician, tree surgeon, and vampire—proving we suffer no lack of imagination!

Pigeonholing designers into limited applications is simply no longer practical. Design skills will find broad use, and embedding design into new arenas will create clear benefits. Trying new things stretches the bounds of designers' creativity. By incorporating the processes and methodologies of other industries, we can help further our own industry in turn. Embedded designers can come from anywhere and do anything, meaning interests we have outside of work can actually define our careers if we let them. We also have a more serious role to play: we can help fix the world's problems. 44

To do this, we may have to ask ourselves some difficult questions, especially in reassessing the value of our current work. But from the very beginning, designers are instilled with a love for creative problem solving; we're taught to understand human behavior, avoid cliché, strive for improvement, and we have honed our ability to effectively communicate. We are equipped to deal with any tough problems. 45

Design holds the ability to disrupt entire industries. Designers will be able to contribute to the sort of change we'd like to see in the world. Such decisions won't be easy; there will be many challenges, but nothing beyond our capabilities. 46

Do Your Homework

Research towards cultural development.

by **Sharlene King**
notepad@tinytank.net, @typodactyl

FEW THINGS ANGER ME MORE than 1
professional inadequacy. In art school, our education heavily relied on critiques. I was vicious in critiques. I drew tears from ill-prepared students who couldn't articulate their work. It was infuriating to have my education affected by students who couldn't bother with our industry's vocabulary; from the day you set foot in a classroom, you bear responsibility for understanding your industry. My peers all chose design, and they should have known and defended their craft.

Being self-righteous wasn't produc- 2
tive, though. My own flaws and weaknesses were obvious to everyone but myself—living by my ego crushed my self-awareness, and I wasn't practicing what I preached.

Homework is *research and practice with* 3
the goal of improvement. Homework isn't client work; it happens outside of your daily practice. Without it, you'll be working in a vacuum, sheltered from any real measurement or development. When you do your homework, you reap

the benefits of competitive knowledge, skills, and the undercurrents of your industry.

Homework in context

Even if we do homework, we may not be doing 4
homework *right*. Homework demonstrates how well we've absorbed a lesson, but usually we simply mimic the lesson to the teacher's liking. Steven Pinker says that intelligence comes from processing accrued information;[1] simply having that information doesn't help you put the pieces together in the long run—and tests may inhibit creativity. Academically, measurement works best when an objective conclusion can be determined, but that makes it hard to accurately measure success in creative fields.[2]

When you haven't done homework in so 5
long, it's easy to presume you've understood something immediately. Likewise, it's easy to believe you know the true nature of your own aesthetic responses. Your shaky preconceptions aren't revealed until you're asked to articulate how and why you reacted the way you did. But practice forms expertise—and it's hard for us to

1. Steven Pinker, *How the Mind Works,* W.W. Norton, 2009, pp. 64–79.
2. Teresa M. Amabile corroborates this in *The Social Psychology of Creativity,* Springer-Verlag, 1983, pp. 142–149 by demonstrating that repeated, rigorous evaluation may not lead to the kind of flexibility in thinking that is needed for a creative mind-set.

measure how good we are. Elliott Jaques made a similar point in his *Creativity and Work*:[3]

> Systematic observation of these issues calls for a special attitude, an attitude of detached involvement, to be achieved only with intense mental toil. By mental toil I mean that creative act in which our conscious beliefs, principles, and concepts are held not as perfect and immutable, as hard-and-fast currency, but as flexible counters, always uncertain and incomplete, and always under scrutiny for modification in light of the reality of experience – concepts, ideas, principles, models, constantly subjected to the modifying influence of common perception.

Jaques argues that we need the objectiv- 6
ity of systematic discipline to create reliable and consistent concepts. Without systematic discipline, your work is just speculative imagination. He further argues that this discipline creates shared perceptions—a collective consciousness—when it's practiced broadly.[4] According to Robert Florida, collective consciousness defines the creative class; your accomplishments hold weight against a community of like-minded people. Without establishing a discipline around our work, it's much

3. Elliott Jaques, *Creativity and Work*, 9th edition, George H. Pollock, 1990, pp. 10–11.

4. *Ibid.*, pp. 9–13.

harder for us to participate in our own field,[5] so we need a way to know that we're improving.

In order to develop your own homework, 7
you need to analyze your own needs and reassess those needs over time. Without knowing where you want to go, you'll only make trivial improvements. Homework without iteration won't help you, either.[6]

Your work needs strong critique in order 8
to improve, and that comes through **constructive criticism**. According to M. Neil Browne, good critical questions may include:[7]

- Are you asking the right questions?
- What makes the answer correct?
- How has your emotional involvement affected your discovery?
- Who cares? Will the uncovered information be valuable to anyone else?
- Do the answers provoke more questions?
- What evidence informs your opinion?

---

5. Robert Florida, *The Rise of the Creative Class*, Basic Books, 2002, pp. 67–82, 88–96.
6. Mike Monteiro and Katie Gillum, *Let's Make Mistakes* #14, "Not Your Friend". http://dsn.tc/02b-02.
7. M. Neil Browne, *Asking the Right Questions: A Guide to Critical Thinking*, 2nd edition, Prentice-Hall, 1981–1986, pp. 1–8. Browne discusses the merits of systematic evaluation and specifically names examples of good critical questions. Being critical isn't about the destruction of an idea, he posits, but elaborating the path of a thought.

- Do you understand the reasons for thc conclusion?
- How are you measuring your success?

We all need solid criticisms. You'll 9
probably be wrong at first—but through criticism and repetition, you'll get closer to being right. Homework involves creation, reaction, conversation, and systematic evaluation—all without client intervention.[8]

What homework means for us

While systematic discipline determines the 10
quality of your homework, it is practiced through repeatedly exercising your skills. Culturally branching out is an exercise in *research*; designing Swiss-influenced punk rock gig posters is an exercise in *practice*.

Swissted is a personal side project of Mike 11
Joyce that redesigns punk rock posters in a strict Swiss style, using simple geometric elements and lowercase Akzidenz-Grotesk to express minimalist concepts.[9] As of this writing, over two hundred posters have been made.

You could argue that Joyce is anti-design, 12
with his generous use of neutral elements on subjects with broad appeal. As a personal project, though, it doesn't have to answer to client concerns or business needs. Swissted is a great example of homework: it's a personal

---

8. *Ibid.*
9. http://www.swissted.com.

side project combining and exploring two passionate interests. As Joyce progresses, his Swissted posters have become more polished and marketable, even though that may not have been the intended goal. Swissted makes Joyce a better designer, more capable of articulating a specific part of his visual language.

Design has many different disciplines, 13
but they all share "the planning and patterning of any act towards a desired, foreseeable end".[10] Success happens when we close the gap between our intentions and the resulting design. Exercise through homework gets us closer to that end goal, no matter our creative passions.

Measurement

In traditional education, a teacher uses grades 14
to communicate how well you understood the curriculum. Outside of an educational setting, grading has a few analogies: professional accomplishments, likes on Dribbble, or maybe a flurry of links to something you've created.

As Jaques describes, systematic observa- 15
tion helps us logically group concepts so we can communicate better with each other.[11] Towards that end, measurement is about *consistency*

---

10. Guy Julier, *The Culture of Design*, 2nd Edition, Sage Publications, 2008, p. 40, quoting Victor Papanek in his book *Design for the Real World*, Academy Chicago, 1972.

11. Elliott Jaques, *Creativity and Work*, pp. 9–13.

in how we communicate: after all, a system of measurement is only reliable if it's consistent.

How can we create objective metrics in 16
a discipline that is so dependent on subjective observation? By relying on each other. That's why the design community is so important. Our work constantly requires cultural assessment and critique for aesthetic and business objectives, and collaboration is the best way to make that happen.[12]

For instance, the portfolio reviews of 17
groups like AIGA, the HOW Conference, and National Portfolio Day Association offer a rudimentary review process—they're short and superficial. Each process is connected to the professional or educational industries—AIGA and HOW's reviewers tend to be in a position to hire you, while NPDA assesses how well you'd perform in a school—but general portfolio reviews rarely connect you with people you end up pursuing professionally.

12. Robert Florida, *The Rise of the Creative Class*, pp. 35, 79, 293–297. Florida expands the discussion to address how the pursuit of diversity is actually self-serving for creatives; when our ideas and talents oppose normative culture, they are typically rejected in a conservative environment; likewise, a liberal workplace is less likely to punish the unconventional. He correlates a diverse environment to the tolerance of creativity. For example, in his research, cities with high family-friendly scores also ranked high with gay people.

These days, though, most designers take to Twitter, Forrst, and Dribbble. For example, I have developed many professional relationships with colleagues on Twitter, and I email them work for critique and discussion. Their answers help provide context to my work, but they don't have a personal stake in any of my projects. They are, however, professional compasses that inspire me. 18

Here in Chicago, 2 Night Stand is a hack weekend[13] organized by design firm Bright Bright Great.[14] Teams end up mentoring each other, whether or not they share the same experiences, disciplines, or talent. Hack weekends prioritize who you work with and how you collectively reach a goal, instead of how you earn a paycheck—which forces a dependency on the process. 19

---

13. 2 Night Stand, http://www.2nightstand.com. Prospective designers send in portfolios, and participants are drawn from the applicants. The organizers attempt to represent a variety of disciplines and styles, and organize everyone into a few small groups, who spend a few days on creative deliverables for a single imaginary client.

14. Bright Bright Great, http://brightbrightgreat.com. *(Full disclosure: Bright Bright Great sponsored this issue without knowing they would be cited, and Sharlene had no knowledge of their sponsorship while writing her essay. —ed.)*

Practice and mistakes

Mistakes are one of the best ways to improve 20
your practice, and some of them have led to great inventions.[15] Homework gives us the freedom to make mistakes; with less pressure on our output, we can be okay with screwing up. The real world often accounts for this, too: if you're editing on Wikipedia, for example, there is a sandbox available so you don't destroy a live article. Interactive agencies and large websites separate their staging sites from production, too.

In David Bayles and Ted Orland's *Art &* 21
Fear, an entire chapter is devoted to discussing the profound lack of control we have over our creative processes.[16] Creative success is built on those who quit before us. We are successful not by talent or intelligence, but by our perseverance. We continue to create because we have learned how to continue—and continuing means we know how not to quit. Practice is an act of endurance; endurance requires you to keep going.

---

15. Many inventions were accidental. Coca-Cola was originally a headache cure; in the pursuit of refrigeration, Roy Plunkett invented Teflon; saccharin was discovered by a scientist who didn't wash his hands after working, and noticed that his food tasted sweeter.
16. David Bayles and Ted Orland, *Art & Fear*, Capra Press, 2000.

Practice has to exist in safe environments, 22
free from responsibility and pressure. As designers, we have to grow our reputation, build our skills, and pay our rent. But while design may depend on bridging the gap between intention and result, we possess a remarkably small amount of control over the whole process. We can control our intentions, but we can't control our audience's or client's responses.[17] Homework frees us from that scrutiny, and that makes us more comfortable with failure.

Ramifications

It's impossible to pinpoint precise cultural shifts: 23
the factors are esoteric and numerous enough to overwhelm most people. Most of us willfully ignore most culture, popular or no, because we may not be interested in the majority of artistic work. It takes effort to actively absorb culture, especially work we don't immediately like; it's much easier to stay comfortable with the things we *do* like. *Art & Fear* describes our collective **conceptual inertia** as so stubborn that we only recognized a round earth when all flat-earth believers died.[18] But research can provide us with valuable cultural insights. We can learn where design practice came from, and that teaches us new ways to work with design going forward.

---

17. *Ibid.*, pp. 9–21.

18. *Ibid.*, p. 57.

Likewise, if you plan on communicating in a relevant way, you can't only listen to the delayed echo of mass culture. Designers are the gatekeepers for communicating culture—whether a gig poster, a coupon for Mac & Cheese, or a new smartphone app. When you wait for cultural change to happen, you cease to be a participant in your own field. 24

As technology improves, we can give more of our time and attention to enjoying culture. That extra attention is referred to as a **cognitive surplus**,[19] which was coined by Clay Shirky in reference to cultural inventions that occupy a populace's time—like London's gin obsession during the Industrial Revolution, as well as the proliferation of reading after the invention of the printing press. 25

For our purposes, the Industrial Revolution isn't much different from the technological revolution we're facing now. Both involve the convergence of millions of people, and both of them bring about a significant shift in our standards of living. Both revolutions needed a way to bring levity: London had gin, we have short jokes on Twitter.[20] 26

In the years before the industrial revolution, mass printing was viewed as a cultural abomination by many intellectuals who didn't 27

---

19. Clay Shirky, *Cognitive Surplus,* Penguin, 2010, pp. 1–12.
20. *Ibid.*

want to see reading brought to the masses.[21] Just as today's intellectuals chide television, video games, and other digital forms of entertainment, earlier intellectuals viewed the proliferation of reading with the same condescending disdain of popularized culture. Edgar Allen Poe declared in 1845:[22]

> The enormous multiplication of books in every branch of knowledge is one of the greatest evils of this age; since it presents one of the most serious obstacles to the acquisition of correct information by throwing in the reader's way piles of lumber in which he must painfully grope for the scraps of useful lumber.

Today, pop culture undermines our ability 28
to measure objective quality. The democratization of measurement leads to inconsistency and corruption; we, too, have to "painfully grope for the scraps of useful lumber." But the core problem changed: the medium doesn't matter as much as our potentially limited viewpoints.

In *The Information Diet*, Clay Johnson says 29
diversity of knowledge supports the integrity of our opinions.[23] Only seeking knowledge that confirms our opinion is the informational

---

21. *Ibid.*, pp. 46–48.
22. Edgar Allan Poe, *Marginalia*, 1840-1849, as quoted in Gorton Carruth and Eugene Ehrlich, *The Harper Book of American Quotations*, Harper & Row, 1988, p. 35.
23. Clay Johnson, *The Information Diet*, O'Reilly, 2012, pp. 113–115.

equivalent of junk food. But junk food is fine to eat sparingly: after all, we'll always bond with like-minded people, and it's certainly more enjoyable to do so. Dependence on that kind of information has a way of corrupting our thinking. Once you lean towards a given bias, you move further from the complex synthesis of personal contribution to a greater society.

Shirky draws many parallels between dif- 30
ferent cultural shifts, positing that our ability to synthesize and address many social contexts defines our creative abilities. Put another way: it isn't how many wheels we can invent, but how many purposes and uses we create for them.[24] We must be critical and analytical if we are to maintain consistent quality in our work. Being critical isn't about the destruction of a given idea, but elaborating on the train of thought behind that idea.[25]

Being analytical is something learned, honed, 31
and then applied. Focus on the habits you need to develop to analyze your own practice.[26]

---

24. Clay Shirky, *Cognitive Surplus,* pp. 184–213. Shirky cites more examples throughout *Cognitive Surplus.*

25. M. Neil Browne, *Asking the Right Questions: A Guide to Critical Thinking,* pp. 1–8.

26. Jessica Hische, "Inspiration vs. Imitation", http://dsn.tc/02b-01. While I'm encouraging critical skills for your overall improvement, Hische says it is also a preventative measure that can help professionally.

This can apply to any field. For instance, if you like music, you can reach out to a community of equally passionate people, be analytical about the music you enjoy, and try to appreciate as many different styles as possible. By doing these three things, you can develop a healthier appetite for what you already love. [27]

Homework's effect on design communities

The Influencers and the Influenced

In 1953, William M. Ivins, Jr. wrote *Prints and Visual Communication* to shed light on the artistic and cultural impact that printmaking left on society. He wrote that visual communication and design wasn't limited to printmaking: [28]

> While the number of printed pictures and designs that have been made as works of art is very large, the number made to convey visual information is many times greater. Thus the story of prints is not, as many people seem to think, that of a minor art form but

27. William Duggan, *Strategic Intuition*, Columbia University Press, 2007, pp. 39–54. Duggan specifically cites the work of psychologist Gary Klein, who developed empirical studies on how experts are able to quickly react in high-pressure situations: for example, the firefighter who senses a backdraft behind a closed door, or a nurse who recognizes when someone is about to go into shock. Intelligent memory allows us to react quickly and instinctively, based on our accrued experiences.
28. William M. Ivins, Jr., *Prints and Visual Communication*, MIT Press, 1953, p. 158.

> that of a most powerful method of communication between men...

For Ivins, printing had cultural impact as a repeated statement. People get informed, and culture progresses, through repeatable communication.[29] In this way, our work is only as valuable as how it's received. The influential share their ideas; the influenced repeat those ideas. The sharing is more important than the inception.

The Professional Undercurrent

We're competitive by nature. We aspire to a higher position within society, and we want to be more capable than our peers. Elliott Jaques studied the social structure of factories and found that their success relied on a successful definition of hierarchy. It wasn't that workers were happily content in their roles; rather, they were given a specific path for improvement. Conversely, if workers weren't given goals and structure, communication and internal relationships quickly broke down. Without

29. *Ibid.*, pp. 1–20.

a point of reference for self-identity, people have no direction for self-growth.[30]

Since the design industry evaluates work 34
in a qualitative way, it often relies on social comparisons. We establish our own perspective by comparing ourselves to one another —giving us recognition, a title, or personal validation. The desire for social dominance is known as our **status imperative**, which has historically provoked conflicts from trivial sibling rivalries to global class wars.[31]

Cultural leaders have always had a tenuous 35
relationship with popular culture: they may *represent* popular culture, but often shirk involvement with those who *consume* popular culture.[32] Because popular culture requires little effort to access, it becomes stigmatized by representing the underclass. Peter Savile once coldly summarized this when he said "cultural

30. Elliot Jaques, *The Changing Culture of a Factory*, Tavistock Publications, 1951, pp. 300–305. Jaques defined role confusion: without a clearly defined hierarchy, workers adopted more responsibilities than they were capable of fulfilling, believing themselves to be higher on the ladder than they really were.
31. David L. Weiner, *Reality Check*, Prometheus Books, 2005, pp. 195–233. For example, a husband might make a demeaning comment to his stay-at-home wife; as a result, the husband takes possession of a positional dominance, and the wife loses power accordingly, forming a rift of inequality between them.
32. For instance, the aforementioned example of Edgar Allen Poe's disdain for popularized reading.

codes are being used to legitimise banality".[33] It takes a lot of work to keep tabs on how culture works, but it's required if you're going to effect any cultural change. Savile's specific grievance is that designers move into art practice without the education of critical analysis: "Artists realize they only have themselves to give, whereas design covers that up all the time."[34]

Similarly, it's common for cultural leaders to 36
disdain the uninitiated. Many famous designers build their own popularity through studying esoteric branches of culture. As cultural leaders amass recognition and attention for their own good work, they distance themselves from those with less cultural reception. It's one of the darker sides of the creative class: we claim a meritocracy, but the quiet elite is protective of their success, and many junior-level designers have more questions than answers.[35] I believe success comes through homework: the projects we do separate from our day-to-day work, that help us *live* design rather than simply *work in* design, allow passionate designers to break through.

---

33. Peter Saville, *Grafik* #159, "Confessions of an Art Defector", p. 69.

34. *Ibid.*, p. 70.

35. Robert Florida, *The Rise of the Creative Class*, pp. 78–79. Florida discuses meritocracy largely in a positive light—mentioning, for instance, its ability to upend a caste system.

A way forward

Design only makes sense in context. Learn to 37
differentiate work culturally and qualitatively. Enjoy everything you love, but be analytical about why you love it.[36] It's okay to like something for its own sake, but you can't use personal taste to justify your work.

You have to practice in order to turn out 38
good work, but you also have to cultivate your knowledge of the difference between good work and bad work. Develop new habits. Make lots of mistakes. Relish those mistakes. Analyze those mistakes and make something better. Don't obsess about any of your successes; you'll stop learning and repeat yourself.

We are each individually responsible for ad- 39
vancing design, so get out of your office and participate. Nobody will carry you along if you aren't already willing to keep up. Homework indulges our inclinations, strengthens our skills,[37] and provides access to an inspirational community.

---

36. M. Neil Browne, *Asking the Right Questions: A Guide to Critical Thinking.*

37. Steven Johnson, *Where Good Ideas Come From,* Riverhead, 2010.

Finding Meaning In the Technium Cave

Blazing trails to benefit society.

by **Francisco Inchauste**
francisco@getfinch.com, @iamFinch

> The cleverer we get, the more 'civilised' we become, the more we seem to hunger for that old sense of mystery that must have brimmed up in us when we looked outside our extraordinary world and understood none of it.[1]

A FEW DAYS BEFORE CHRISTMAS 1994, 1
three explorers were searching for caves in the Ardèche, a region in Southern France. They found an updraft of cool air near the edge of a cliff, cleared some rubble, and found a passage—barely large enough for a person to climb through. The smallest member of the

1. Quote is from Waldemar Januszczak, *The Guardian*, 3 Dec 1998. Found in Alan Fletcher, *The Art of Looking Sideways*, Phaidon Press, 2001, p. 15.

group was able to squeeze through first, and they all soon fit through a larger opening.[2,3]

Although the cave was beautiful, nothing 2
stood out at first. But as the three friends reached a deeper part, one of them called out: "They have been here!"[4] With those words, the explorers had become the first humans in 20,000 years to gaze upon "the Sistine Chapel of the Upper Paleolithic", marking one of the most notable archaeological discoveries in history.[5]

Lost in translation

Made with crushed hematite and Scotch pine, 3
the Paleolithic paintings in Chauvet-Pont-d'Arc Cave are twice older than any other known. They were preserved when the main entrance of the cave was sealed in by a landslide. Very few people are allowed to see them, due to the pathogens that could be brought into this extremely fragile environment.[6] But inside is a fascinating snapshot of

---

2. Werner Herzog, *Cave of Forgotten Dreams,* 25 Mar 2011. http://dsn.tc/02c-10.
3. Judith Thurman, "First Impressions", *The New Yorker,* 23 Jun 2008. http://dsn.tc/02c-09.
4. *Ibid.*
5. Matthew Campbell, "Paleolithic 'Sistine Chapel' Finally Set to See the Light, via Proxy", *The Australian,* 20 Jun 2011. http://dsn.tc/02c-05.
6. Waldemar Januszczak, "Werner Herzog Unveils the Deep and Meaningful", *The Australian,* 30 Mar 2011, http://dsn.tc/02c-06.

prehistoric life, with traces of tools, meals, and footprints left in the soft clay ground.[7]

Cavemen are popularly depicted as slow- 4
witted and unimaginative, but these drawings provide an early glimpse of human creativity. The cave paintings include horses, lions, rhinos, and geometric shapes (arguably an early writing system), but one thing is typically absent: a full human form.[8] For our ancestors, these caves posed a significant danger, so why would they risk a journey to leave these markings?

And what did they mean? Without any 5
cultural context or a language to translate, we will likely never know. Whatever the motivation, though, this yearning to create is part of who we were, and part of who we are. It's what makes us human. The cave art was potentially a way to control something in an world that seemed so uncontainable. We find similar feelings (although much less risky) with the internet and the future of our creations in it. Once we let something into the wild, it becomes something new. Frank Chimero says, "[The initial creator's] work will be used to say and

7. Werner Herzog, *Cave of Forgotten Dreams.*

8. The only human-esque drawing found in the cave was a human-animal hybrid. These figures are sometimes called "sorcerers" and represent the human taking form of an "avatar" or "animal spirit". See also Dr. Jean Clottes, "Paleolithic Cave Art in France", Bradshaw Foundation, http://dsn.tc/02c-08.

do things they don't intend. Ideas, in truth, go further when others carry them, and this usually means they will go in directions the original author did not intend or imagine."[9]

Living, more or less

32,000 years later, we express ourselves in 6
numerous ways. While our creative intentions are probably quite distant from the intentions of our ancestors, we still strive to create meaningful pieces of ourselves. Instead of writing in caves, we communicate through what Kevin Kelly calls *the technium*: a cultural and technological system with thousands of years of precedent. The technium is an ecosystem with a behavior of its own, larger than the sum of modern art, social institutions, and intellectual concepts.[10]

Take your smartphone, for example. You 7
couldn't create that on your own, even if your smartest friends were able to help. Thousands of separate technologies had to be invented before we could mass-produce smartphones. Without the technium, that phone would not be possible to create, maintain, or use—and now we are dependent on and defined by it.[11]

---

9. Comment by Frank Chimero in article by Danuel Howells, "Svbtle vs Obtvse (and on copying)", 23 Mar 2012. http://dsn.tc/02c-07.
10. Kevin Kelly, *What Technology Wants*, Viking Adult, 2010. http://dsn.tc/02c-04.
11. *Ibid.*

In examining what's being created today, we 8
find a disconnect between us and the things we desire. We want things to be authentic, but they usually fall short. Software's design provides only metaphor, with hints of paper texture and inked draft lines to feel more tactile. Instead of meeting someone for coffee, we "like" their status about drinking their first cup in the morning. Taken to extremes, one's digital life can pull apart their real life, as seen in Alice Gregory's numbing essay "Sad As Hell":[12]

> You really want to know what it is about 20-somethings? It's this: we live longer now. But we also live less. It sounds hyperbolic, it sounds morbid, it sounds dramatic, but in choosing the internet I am choosing not to be a certain sort of alive. Days seem over before they even begin, and I have nothing to show for myself other than the anxious feeling that I now know just enough to engage in conversations I don't care about.

Meanwhile, you might think that 9
Jaron Lanier, a technology visionary who coined the term "virtual reality," would be excited by the technium, but he doesn't see all of it as a good thing:[13]

---

12. Alice Gregory, "Sad as Hell", *n+1*, 9 Nov 2010. http://dsn.tc/02c-02.
13. Jaron Lanier, "You Are Not a Gadget", TEDx San Francisco, 2010. http://dsn.tc/02c-03.

> I'm concerned that we're all fitting more and more into more database representations of ourselves. I'm concerned that we're letting algorithms recommend friends, music, and movies to us, in a way that is separating us from each other.

As any new medium develops, it ini- 10
tially harbors enthusiasts and skeptics. With the internet, we praised the abundance of digital tools, but lamented our dwindling attention. Our options to communicate, share, and consume ideas rival that of science fiction, but our detractors see us as narcissistic, praising of mediocrity.[14]

Marshall McLuhan ignored the content of 11
the mediums, focusing instead on how new mediums changed the way we think and act.[15] But not even McLuhan could have predicted the effects of the internet. We have an insatiable appetite for information. We compulsively

---

14. Nicholas Carr, *The Shallows: What the Internet Is Doing to Our Brains*, W. W. Norton, 2010, pp. 2–3. http://dsn.tc/02c-01.
15. *Ibid.*

check for updates.[16] As Nicholas Carr says, "The Net's interactivity gives us powerful new tools for finding information, expressing ourselves, and conversing with others. It also turns us into lab rats constantly pressing levers to get tiny pellets of social or intellectual nourishment."[17]

As the technium expands, it changes our 12
frame. For example, our concept of time used to be more relaxed; we measured it based on cues from nature; when the sun rose and set. After the mechanical clock was invented, though, we split up our days, micromanaged our tasks, and soon became "busy" clock watchers, obsessed with the increments of time. What began as non-invasive came to run our lives. As the clock became small enough to fit in our pockets or on our wrists, it became more personal—a sort of "Big Brother"

---

16. Various studies show us that the Internet is actually changing how we think. When we read online, certain parts of our mind are activated—excited, even. This kind of thought is much different from when we are reading a book or newspaper. We don't know exactly how this will affect our brains or cognition in the long term, but we do know it is doing something. See also Nicholas Carr, *The Shallows: What the Internet Is Doing to Our Brains*. Or, if you prefer online, his excellent essay in *The Atlantic*, "Is Google Making Us Stupid?", available at http://dsn.tc/02c-20.

17. Nicholas Carr, *The Shallows: What the Internet Is Doing to Our Brains*, p. 117.

always reminding us of the exact volume of time we had spent or had left to spend.[18]

Now we compare our thinking to the way 13
computers work. We explain our memories in terms of how a machine accesses and writes information. Even the language we use to explain our thinking includes terms like "hard-wired", reflecting the physical constructs of a computer.[19] It's almost impossible to leave the technium we've created. It is gravity, an invisible force holding us in place. When something in the technium changes, we change with it.

The failure of intended innovation

We like to believe we can control the way 14
innovation plays out—and that it can happen in a linear, repeatable way. We try to find patterns in overnight successes. But business book fodder isn't how innovation really happens.

Before Silicon Valley became the role model 15
for our work, most of our productive output tried to change things in smaller ways. Many influential inventions came from intentions for something much simpler, and grew into something essential. For example, in 1880, the United States had an influx of so many immigrants that it took eight years to complete the census—and the next one would fare even worse. The census hired a young engineer, Herman Hollerith, to

---

18. *Ibid.*, pp. 41–44.

19. *Ibid.*, p. 23.

find a way to automate the process of gathering data. Inspired by the automatic loom, Hollerith devised a way to punch cards in specific positions to represent the data of each citizen: sex, age, date of birth, etc. With these punch card-reading machines in place for 1890's census, it was completed at twice the speed. Shortly after, Hollerith's punch cards were employed in the world's first computers. He had stumbled upon the basic binary language that all future computers would eventually run on.[20]

Ideas are incremental; we build off of what 16
came before. True innovation, then, refers more to an idea's impact, not the idea itself. Nobody can control the effect that an idea has on the world; influence can only be determined in hindsight. Scott Berkun points out that seemingly small changes could be disruptive:[21]

---

20. See James Burke, *Connections*, Macmillan London, 1976, pp. 112–113. James Burke also created a documentary television series for the BBC in 1978 called "Connections," which explored the unexpected ways that our modern world and its technology came to be, through tracing the path back through to the point of origin. The entire series is available on YouTube at http://dsn.tc/02c-17.

21. Scott Berkun, "Does Size Matter for Ideas?", *Harvard Business Review*, 5 Oct 2010. http://dsn.tc/02c-18.

> There's a myth at work here: the assumption that big results only come from radical changes. There's good evidence for a counter-argument. The problems that plague organizations, or hold them back from greatness, are often small things that happen to be consistently overlooked. The lack of progress or greatness isn't because there's a grand idea missing. Instead the cause is a simple idea prevented by bureaucracy, killed out of ignorance, or buried under incompetence. If those simpler, smaller, ideas were set free, the effect would be as potent as any grand theory.

In a paper coauthored by Don Norman and Robert Verganti, they break down the differences in two types of innovation: Incremental and Radical. Incremental being a small series of improvements to a current solution, and radical being something that has not been done before (Think: iPhone versus every cell phone before it). They argue that these are reached by two separate methods. They use the hill-climbing paradigm to explain the difference between the two types of innovations:

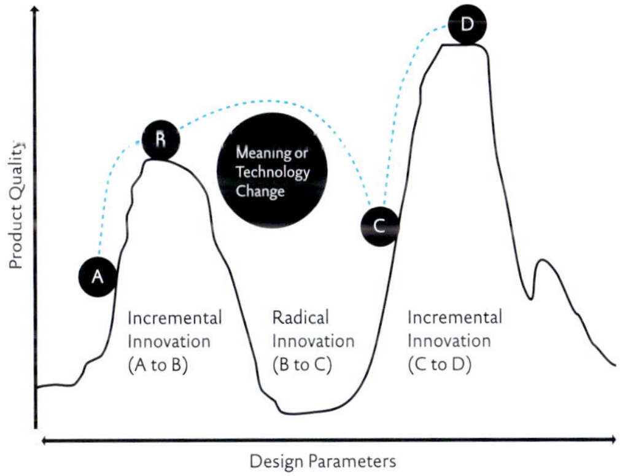

A given product might start off at "A." Through Human-Centered Design and Design Research (HCD & DR), the product undergoes a series of incremental innovations, eventually bringing it to its maximum quality for this part of the design space, point "B." To move to a different hill, one with a higher potential, requires radical innovation, and this comes about through either technology or meaning change, leading to point "C" on a larger hill. Note that the initial outcome is often inferior to that previously reached ("B"), and so HCD and DR are required to make the necessary incremental innovations to reach maximum potential. To make matters more complex, when the product is at point "C," there is no way of knowing if indeed there is a superior level ("D") or if this is an inferior spot in the design space.[22]

22. Donald A. Norman and Roberto Verganti, "Incremental and Radical Innovation: Design Research Versus Technology and Meaning Change", 18 Mar 2012. http://dsn.tc/02c-19.

In his own investigations, Norman found 18
that every example of radical innovation was not reached through design research. This includes technology that came before the advent of design research—inventions like electric lighting and the automobile—all the way through to ones that came after it—social networks like Twitter or Facebook. These ideas came about because the inventors were simply interested in trying them out.

Verganti also found that not only was tech- 19
nology a driver of radical change, but it could also arrive through a change in meaning. His research is rooted in several definitions of design, including this one from John Heskett:[23]

> Design [is] the deliberate and reasoned shaping and making of our environment in ways that satisfy our needs and give meaning to our lives.

When we think about innovation, we're really describing *radical* innovation—which is comparatively quite rare. Big ideas often start small, and the world is influenced slowly. For example, Apple didn't invent the multi-touch interface; it had been around for over 20 years before the introduction of the iPhone. But they introduced the technology in a meaningful way, causing the *perception* of radical innovation.[24]

---

23. *Ibid.*

24. *Ibid.*

But we still glamorize the creative process, 20
sell it as calculated and repeatable, and hope for grandiose products that will change the world. Reality is more modest. As shown in the research by Verganti and Norman, successful design gave meaning to people by definition.

Startup stagnation

We are in an era of planned obsolescence. 21
Factories work feverishly to produce the latest hardware, with a human cost that we've inadvertently built in.[25] And if you aren't involved in a startup of some sort, then what are you doing with your life? The rewards seem within easy reach. Some are even investing in *nothing*—funding teams without a product in mind yet—in the slim chance it will actually become *something*.[26] It's the lottery for the technologically savvy—but if played right, whole industries can be redefined, and genuine value can be created for everyone.

---

25. In a series of articles called *The iEconomy, The New York Times* examined the globalization of the high-tech industry and the challenges in producing the "iThings" that we so love by focusing on workers' mental and physical health problems. For more, see Charles Duhigg and David Barboza, "In China, Human Costs are Built into an iPad", *The New York Times*, 25 Jan 2012. http://dsn.tc/02c-15.

26. Jeff Bercovici, "Silicon Valley's Hottest New Start-Up Idea: Nothing", *Forbes*, 26 Apr 2012. http://dsn.tc/02c-16.

Right now, many disruptive companies are 22
just beginning their life. We look to startups because when corporations grow to a certain point, it's hard for them to adapt to customers' needs. With the *Innovator's Dilemma* we find many established companies that reach the top of their game and then suddenly fall flat on their face; finding out the hard way that there is indeed a difference in drive for profit and growth versus creating value or meaning. They are unable to catch up with other companies that have embraced a market or technology that they never saw as profitable, and by proxy, a threat.[27]

However, many startups pursue disrup- 23
tion and profit, only to find the same fate as their failed peers. Dave Kashen describes the process:[28]

> In the startup world, thousands of entrepreneurs focus their ingenuity on finding ways to make millions of dollars. They look for market inefficiencies and focus on questions like: "Will consumers pay for this?" without asking "Will this make people's lives meaningfully better?" It's not that we shouldn't try to

---

27. *The Innovator's Dilemma* is a book that "deeply influenced" Steve Jobs. He is one of the only CEOs to have led a company to successfully beat this conundrum. See also James Allworth, "Steve Jobs Solved the Innovator's Dilemma", *Harvard Business Review*, 24 Oct 2011. http://dsn.tc/02c-14.
28. Dave Kashen, "The Values-Driven Startup", *GigaOM*, 17 Dec 2011. http://dsn.tc/02c-12.

make money, it's just that money should be merely one of many factors we strive for, and it's played far too central a role for far too long.

Amy Hoy looks at the cost of burnout for those involved:[29]

> Every fucking time you see somebody using glory to hagiographize young men & women who are doing something clearly stupid, you must ask:
>
> *What is this raft of shit, and why are they trying to get me to paddle it?*
>
> And make no mistake, bartering away your "one and only youth" working 100-hour weeks on a web site for the promise of a big fat carrot on the end of a stick 80 million lines long, dangled by a fat statesm–venture capitalist, who will make 3x or 10x or 100x more than you, in the vanishingly unlikely scenario that you "succeed"... is clearly stupid.

With the explosion of aspirational "startup porn"[30] like Pinterest and a continuous flow of new iThings, we have bought into the illusion—"artificially created demand"[31]—that consuming products and rampant innovation is propelling us toward a better life. And creating digital

29. Amy Hoy, "Fuck Glory—Startups Are One Long Con", *Unicorn Free*, 29 Nov 2011. http://dsn.tc/02c-13.
30. Cennydd Bowles, "The Things of the Future", *Update 2011*, 5 Sept 2011. http://dsn.tc/02c-11.
31. *Ibid.*

wares is appealing because it seems like creating new jobs would be good for our economy—but digital landfills are problematic, too, with issues arising around archiving and longevity.[32]

Even if there are young companies with 24
meaningful intentions, not all investors are biting. They're looking for ideas that fit existing trends, and they push for a quick exit via acquisition or further funding. Entrepreneur and investor Chris Dixon explains:[33]

> The problem I encounter is that many of these "meaningful" startups have trouble raising money from VCs. An entrepreneur working on groundbreaking robot technology recently joked to me that he'd have an easier time raising money if his robots were virtual and existed only on Facebook.

The truth is, we may well be in the largest 25
slowdown of technological growth in human history. Economist Tyler Cowen calls this the "great stagnation". Take our modern-day kitchen, for example. The 19th-century kitchen was built around a live fireplace, but then we rapidly benefited from electricity,

---

32. For more on information longevity and our civilization's need to save everything, see Jeremy Keith's talk "All Our Yesterdays": http://dsn.tc/02c-26.

33. Chris Dixon, "'Meaningful' startups", cdixon.org, 18 Apr 2012. http://dsn.tc/02c-30.

water, and gas stoves. Then the past fifty years brought no major technological changes.[34]

Silicon Valley investor and web browser inventor Marc Andreessen famously said, "Software is eating the world."[35] He thinks our economy is being revolutionized by computing; our most favored jobs are shifting from the industrial age to the information age:[36]

> This is the great sweep of economic history. When the vast majority of the workforce was in agriculture, it was impossible to imagine what all those people would do if they didn't have agricultural jobs. Then a hundred years later the vast majority of the workforce was in industrial jobs, and we were similarly blind: It was impossible to imagine what workers would do without those jobs.

Even if Andreessen's prediction is right, our current technological trajectory is still far from perfect. From Cowen's perspective, personal computing hasn't broadly improved society's standard of living. He says we've "plucked all the low-hanging fruit". Today, innovation

---

34. Paul Solman, "The Great Stagnation: Why Hasn't Recent Technology Created More Jobs?", *PBS*, 18 May 2011. http://dsn.tc/02c-25.
35. Marc Andreessen, "Why Software Is Eating The World", *The Wall Street Journal*, 20 Aug 2011. http://dsn.tc/02c-28.
36. Chris Anderson, "Software Will Eat the World", *Wired*, 24 Apr 2012. http://dsn.tc/02c-27.

takes more effort. Some of the most successful technology companies haven't done much for job growth: "Take the ubiquitous iPod. It's created less than 14,000 jobs in the U.S., Internet giant Google, 20,000 employees, Twitter, a mere 300."[37] In fact, the net creation rate of jobs has been on the decline since the 1970's.[38]

We're now faced with *consumption-biased technological change*:[39] "technology that benefits mainly the highly skilled workers, but hurts the less-skilled, average person."[40] For those in information jobs, it's an exciting time. Growth and jobs are plentiful. For those outside, though, their quality of life isn't near as great, and it hasn't improved much over the past few decades. The median income has stagnated, we're mainly adding "McJobs" to the economy, and close to half of US is in a *very* fragile financial state—which is a "visible symptom of Great Depression–era level inequality". We're also seeing a "dumbification" of society, where media

37. Paul Solman, "The Great Stagnation: Why Hasn't Recent Technology Created More Jobs?"
38. Umair Haque, "GDP Needs Help: Let's Build a Second Measure of Economic Strength", *The Atlantic*, 3 Jan 2012. http://dsn.tc/02c-29.
39. Bryan Caplan, "Consumption-Biased Technological Change", *Library of Economics and Liberty*, 19 May 2011. http://dsn.tc/02c-24.
40. Paul Solman, "The Great Stagnation: Why Hasn't Recent Technology Created More Jobs?"

misinforms and more people seem to be aware of what's happening on reality TV, than in reality.[41]

Yet, exciting new products are released every 28
day that promise to improve our lives. Are they fulfilling that promise? Are *we*? We make outlandish claims—like one brand of chewing gum will help you get a kiss from a beautiful woman—in order to differentiate. Umhair Haque says this is an industrial age model of product creation: "We have to move from differentiation, to actually making a difference—to people, communities, and societies. Mattering in human terms. I think the key words, when it comes to making a difference, are: human potential."[42] In short, if software is truly eating the world, then it needs to be more meaningful.

Road to Eudaimonia

If a macroeconomist were to best describe 29
the state of our economy, it would look a bit like this: "output equals consumption, plus government expenditure, plus investment, plus net exports". This is also known as the Gross Domestic Product (GDP), the "national income statement" for the United States.

---

41. Umair Haque, "Seven Problems a Recovery Won't Fix", *Harvard Business Review*, 8 Jun 2011. http://dsn.tc/02c-21.
42. Umair Haque, "Why Meaningful Brands Will Matter", Havas Media Labs. http://dsn.tc/02c-23.

The GDP defines basic human exchange through measuring our industrial output.[43]

GDP is a measurement that affects all of our 30
lives. As an aspirational society, we seek bigger, faster, and cheaper material things to create meaning for ourselves. We signify our own prosperity, and that creates envy in our peers. McDonald's offers a perfect example of this: it wasn't enough to have so many options on their menu, all of which are available on demand—so, they gave us the "Super Size" meal.[44] These meals gave us more food than we needed, and the remainder was frequently discarded. Our lust for gratuitous satiation brought us fuel-thirsty SUVs, junk bonds, and a too-perfect green lawn—and we can't afford most of it.

We measure our busyness with things like 31
percentages and Gantt charts in an attempt to provide the short-term feeling of profitability,

---

43. These quotations are from Umar Haque, "GDP Needs Help: Let's Build a Second Measure of Economic Strength".

44. McDonald's Super Size was originally called *Dino-Size* when it was introduced as a movie promotion for Jurassic Park in 1993. They decided to continue the sizes after the original promotion and changed the name to *Super Size*. This ran until 2004 when they began to phase it out—around the time the documentary *Super Size Me* premiered.

rather than actually making a long-term impact:[45]

> [...] what if the firm was driven, not by the goal of short-term profitability, but by the goal of continuous innovation in service of finding new ways of delighting customers? The new bottom line of this kind of organization becomes whether the customer is delighted (e.g. as measured by the Net Promoter Score). Conventional financial measures such as maximizing shareholder value are subordinated to the new bottom line. Profit is a result, not a goal.

Thinking about all of this led me to consider 32
Eudaimonia, a key concept in Aristotelian ethics that loosely translates to *human flourishing.*[46] According to Aristotle, it is a means of "living well" that goes against our usual preconceptions. Normally, we're led to easy answers: wealth, a nice home, great friends, a healthy family, and so on. But happiness doesn't necessarily reside in material possessions; it comes from something more meaningful: "The good of a human being must have something to do with being human; and what sets humanity off from other species, giving us the potential to live a better life, is our capacity to guide our-

45. Steve Denning, "Clayton Christensen and the Innovators' Smackdown", *Forbes*, 5 Apr 2012. http://dsn.tc/02c-22.

46. John M. Cooper, *Reason and Human Good in Aristotle*, Hackett, 1975. http://dsn.tc/02c-38.

selves by using reason. If we use reason well, we live well as human beings; or, to be more precise, using reason well over the course of a full life is what happiness consists in."[47]

In short, it's not about more things: it's about *fewer, better things*. Umair Haque corroborates this: "Its purpose is not merely passive, slack-jawed 'consuming' but living: doing, achieving, fulfilling, becoming, inspiring, transcending, creating, accomplishing—all the stuff that matters the most."[48] We can apply Eudaimonia to the things we make: a Eudiamonic product helps others flourish, no matter what they do. Alan Fletcher makes a similar point:[49]

> Soon we will end up unable to distinguish between the synthetic and the real stuff. Come to think of it, the other day I had a soya bacon sandwich and couldn't tell the difference. However, life is not a technological ladder, it's more of a cultural wheel. So, what we've gained in some respects we have lost in others.

47. Richard Kraut, "Aristotle's Ethics", *The Stanford Encyclopedia of Philosophy*, Spring 2012 Edition. http://dsn.tc/02c-42.
48. Umair Haque, "Is a Well-Lived Life Worth Anything?", *Harvard Business Review*, 12 May 2011. http://dsn.tc/02c-40.
49. Alan Fletcher, *The Art of Looking Sideways*, Phaidon Press, 2001, p. 14.

Although there isn't yet a good method to measure how Eudaimonic a product is, we should consider some qualitative heuristics to help us judge what makes a product meaningful: 34

- It has a **purpose.** A product with purpose means more than its functionality. The purpose of a product is built into its soul, guiding what it can become. Some products are used for their full purpose from day one. Others start out as something else: sometimes looking more like a toy, until their true purpose is discovered by the user. For example, Twitter began as a novel status update service, and—largely due to user intervention—has now become a transformative force in communication.[50] 35
- It enhances **belief**. If you've ever been on an impersonal, robotic customer service call, you've most likely encountered the opposite of this. Companies like shoe retailer Zappos believe in what they are doing—and they treat their customers in kind. We should believe that the customer will truly be better off with what we make—but not many of us can say this confidently. 36
- It's built in **moderation**. The goal of many startups is to be the world's next big thing. What about being the next big thing to a small group? What about crafting something that 37

50. Chris Dixon, "The Next Big Thing Will Start Out Looking Like a Toy", cdixon.org, 3 Jan 2010. http://dsn.tc/02c-39.

innovates in a specific niche? Consider the web industry—and the growing number of intimate conferences like Brooklyn Beta, created partly in response to the massive, catch-all SXSW. It's easier to connect with something that's made for a small group, rather than something that tries to be everything for everyone.

- It follows **human goals**. Not all things 38
are meant to be mass-produced without regard to the human or environmental costs. We can all see the damage we cause when we disregard sustainability, so we need to reevaluate what we stand to gain from anything we put into the world.
- It is **virtuous.** In Greek, the word *virtu* means 39
excellence. Some human virtues include prudence, courage, and justice. In terms of a product, though, virtue informs how it is created and used. For example, Joel Britton defines the qualities of an effective knife: "a good knife cuts well; the virtues by which it reaches this end might include durability, solid construction, a good edge, and so on." Good products strive to be the best they can be, rather than to simply benefit the maker with quick profits.[51]

Now that we have some loose guide- 40
lines for this kind of product, how do we go about making one? Are there any products

51. Joel Britton, "Eudaimonia and the Cardinal Virtues", *Eudaimoniac: Living the Good Life,* 27 Jan 2009. http://dsn.tc/02c-37.

that are meaningful, according to our definition of a Eudaimonic product?

Building meaningful things

The business world constantly discusses 41
how to manufacture success—figuring out what factors can provide the same results as another successful business. Some people take this to extremes, leading to "process cults".[52] In the startup world, one such process cult is the "lean startup" movement, outlined in *The Lean Startup* by Eric Ries.

One of the book's key terms is a **Minimum** 42
Viable Product (MVP), or the smallest product that can succeed in a market. According to Ries,[53] "MVP is designed not to just answer product design or technical questions. Its goal is to test fundamental business hypotheses." Others describe MVP as a "reinvention of user-centered design practice" that's more in line with marketing than design.[54] John Kolko thinks an MVP treats users as "collateral damage" on the way to creating the real product:[55]

---

52. Alex Payne, "On Business Madness", al3x.net, 12 Feb 2012. http://dsn.tc/02c-41.
53. Eric Ries, *The Lean Startup*, Crown Business, 2011, p. 94.
54. Quote by Janice Frasier in article by Jon Kolko, "Collateral Damage: The Ethics of Lean UX", *Austin Center for Design*, 20 Apr 2012. http://dsn.tc/02c-32.
55. *Ibid.*

> "And for all the conversation about 'get out of the building' in order to talk to users and validate your ideas, the tone of the [MVP] process seems to force us back to the smarminess of marketing, but under the guise of science. It's co-opted language that seeks to prove that people will pay for things, and while these may be important for all sorts of various reasons, they don't mesh with design."

It's relatively easy to determine whether 43
products succeed within an MVP framework.[56] But if we turned our focus to creating more meaningful things, we could create a **Minimum Meaningful Product (MMP)** instead.

To start, we need to **choose better** 44
problems. As Mike Monteiro says, we are using amazing tools and technology "to build shit". Our aim has to be higher: "Let's find problems to solve that actually improve people's lives… there has got to be something more beneficial to society than the next Facebook clone."[57]

Many problems simply haven't been tackled 45
yet. The problem is **schlep blindness,** which Paul Graham describes: "Schlep was originally a Yiddish word but has passed into general use in the US. It means a tedious, unpleasant task." Startups should solve more complicated

---

56. Eric *Ries, The Lean Startup*, p. 85.
57. Mike Monteiro, "10 New Year's Resolutions for Designers", *.net Magazine*, 3 Jan 2012. http://dsn.tc/02c-33.

problems in underserved industries.[58] These generally involve a higher proportion of difficult problems to solve—and most people avoid them, because the solutions involve too much work. Simple is trying to revolutionize banking. In their words, "We started Simple because retail banks have forgotten who their customers are."[59] Banking infrastructure isn't easy to build: security issues, ATM networks, and international transfers all sound nightmarish to many of us. But Simple is on its way to make it happen.

Other issues have global scope, known to some as **wicked problems**:[60] dwindling energy supply, education, or healthcare. They seem insurmountable, and they definitely aren't as fun as making the next Pinterest or Twitter—but they need to be solved, too. For example, Tesla Motors is not your average Silicon Valley startup. One of the goals of its CEO, Elon Musk, is to "move us off of fucking oil as fast as possible". If starting a new automobile company is "probably the hardest thing in the world", building an affordable electric car is even crazier. Tesla is creating

58. Paul Graham, "Schlep Blindness", paulgraham.com. http://dsn.tc/02c-36.
59. See the "Vision" section of https://www.simple.com.
60. See also Jon Kolko, *Wicked Problems: Problems Worth Solving*, which talks about the ways design can help major global problems, and the struggles we might face when we try to tackle them. Available online for free at https://www.wickedproblems.com.

one of the first mass-produced electric vehicles (EVs), where most competitors are adaptations of vehicles built with gas-burning technology.[61]

Schlep blindness also breeds an igno- 47
rance of your own customers. For example, most companies want to automate their documentation and support. If you hate yelling numbers at your phone in public, what makes you think your own customers will like it? Minimum Viable Products don't account for the customer experience; a Minimum Meaningful Product has to put the customer at its core.

We've become great at making beauti- 48
ful and usable products, but we've forgotten to forge a lasting, intimate connection with our customers. If people don't think you care about them, they leave—and customers generally value this over price and quality.[62]

How many startups have personally con- 49
tacted you after signing up? Intercom would like to see that happen more often. They are building a customer relationship management (CRM) tool that helps primarily "software as a service" (SaaS) companies to build stronger, more meaningful relationships with their customers. They

---

61. Jon Gertner, "Why Tesla Motors Is Betting on the Model S", *Fast Company*, 19 Mar 2012. http://dsn.tc/02c-31.

62. Des Traynor, "Taking a Customer from Like to Love: The UX of Long-Term Relationships", *Smashing Magazine*, Aug 2011. http://dsn.tc/02c-34.

believe that talking to your customers is the bare minimum in building meaningful relationships. Intercom COO Des Traynor explains:

> Website owners are disconnected from their customers, save for a conference party or survey each year. If you asked them to introduce you to 10 of their customers, most would struggle, grimace and then get a developer to break out the SQL. Imagine trying to run a bar, convenience store, hair salon—heck, any service—with that level of apathy towards the folks who pay your wages.[63]

Meaningful designs must be relevant 50
to your customers. When we build for ourselves, we're following **designer myopia**.[64] So many of today's products serve a scene that celebrates itself, yet designers comprise less than "one-half of one percent" of the world.[65] These kinds of products might be inspirational for those of us who pay attention to such details, but meaningful products aren't necessarily a matter of better design.

Where will your product end up? Creating 51
a sustainable product is important to a meaningful vision. Sustainable products should

63. *Ibid.*

64. Rian van der Merwe, "Designer Myopia: How To Stop Designing for Ourselves", *Smashing Magazine*, 14 Feb 2012. http://dsn.tc/02c-35.

65. Jon Bell, 'HIVE 2011: Make it Relevant", Hive Conference, 2011. http://dsn.tc/02c-50.

have modular architecture, reusable components, and long-term durability. For example, Puma designed a new shoebox called "The Clever Little Bag", a cardboard and cloth bag[66] that is much more sustainable than your typical shoebox. Not only did the new design save paper and energy, but they discovered customers loved the bag and kept using it.

It's difficult to build something that focuses on delight, not profit. It's also hard to measure emotion and trust once something has been released. If you look at companies that listen to their customers and focus on a desirable experience, you'll find customers who evangelize the company and its products. The Net Promoter Score (NPS) is considered the "most practical single measure of customer delight"[67] —and Apple, presently the world's largest company by market capitalization, has some of the

66. "Clever Little Bag", Puma.com. http://dsn.tc/02c-49.

67. Companies needed a better way to determine customer satisfaction and also provide accountability for it. Fred Reichheld and Bain & Company found that one question worked well for "mature, competitive industries": *What is the likelihood that you would recommend Company X to a friend or colleague?* This question was accurate in predicting behaviors like "repurchases, referrals and other actions that contribute to a company's growth". So, out of that research the *Net Promoter Score* was born. See also http://dsn.tc/02c-47.

highest scores of any business sector.[68] Their focus on customer service has served them well, with Apple Stores averaging roughly six times the national average per square foot.[69]

Meaningful design is a lofty goal, but our 53
current product environment is not sustainable. We can't rely on capturing user data and advertising anymore. People will pay for something to ensure that it lasts,[70] and product developers want to be directly paid by their customers.

Millennials have different expectations than 54
other generations. They are known as the "most civic-minded generation since World War II" and the "most socially conscious consumers to date". They demand more of the places they work, the items they consume, and the companies they buy from. For example, 83% say they will trust a company more if it is "socially [or] environmentally responsible". Meanwhile, social media has given them a strong voice—and

68. Steve Denning, "Another Myth Bites the Dust: How Apple Listens To Its Customers", *Forbes*, 26 Aug 2011. http://dsn.tc/02c-46.

69. "Where a typical electronics store averages $1,200 per square foot in sales, mature Apple stores exceed $6,000 per square foot." *Ibid.*

70. "Don't be a free user", *Pinboard Blog*, 6 Dec 2001. http://dsn.tc/02c-48.

they aren't afraid to use it. Products in our future will have to be different to survive.[71]

The future explorers

What we create today will become the baseline for future generations. In the future, explorers will find our technium cave, filled with the artifacts of our present. What will they find in there? What will our creations tell them about what was meaningful to us? I can only hope it's not what I see today. I know it can change, and I hope you see it too.

> When you grow up, you tend to get told that the world is the way it is, and your life is just to live your life inside the world. Try not to bash into the walls too much. Try to have a nice family life. Have fun, save a little money. That's a very limited life. Life can be much broader, once you discover one simple fact, and that is everything around that you call life was made up by people who were no smarter than you. And you can change it. You can influence it. You can build your own things that other people can use. Once you learn that, you'll never be the same again.[72]

---

71. *The 2006 Cone Millennial Cause Study*, Cone, Inc. and AMP Insights. http://dsn.tc/02c-45.
72. Steve Jobs, in the PBS documentary *Steve Jobs: One Last Thing*, whose site is at http://dsn.tc/02c-44. The clips shown were from a previously un-aired interview done in 1995 by Santa Clara Valley Historical Association, while he was still at NeXT, and shortly after he was diagnosed with cancer. An excerpt can be seen at http://dsn.tc/02c-43.

About the authors

Nick Disabato helps other people make *Distance*. He once made *Cadence & Slang*, a very small book about interaction design; and he also founded The Publication Standards Project, an advocacy organization for a saner and more humane digital publishing landscape. An interaction designer by trade, he cares about the way that we talk with each other, and he wants to make our conversations more constructive and meaningful. He can usually be found on his bike somewhere in Chicago.

Cassie McDaniel is a designer at University Health Network in Toronto. She blogs regularly about the murky intersection of healthcare and design in what is probably a lame attempt to get other designers to join the healthcare cause. You can also find her speaking at various events, on Twitter sharing favorite discoveries, or making some kind of to-do list. You will rarely find her doing nothing (if you do, call for help). She has previously been published in *Freelance Switch*, *Smashing Magazine,* and *A List Apart*.

Sharlene King is a designer living in Chicago with two cats, a partner, and a fantastically large collection of matchbooks. She designs on the weekend, in the after hours, and with a mouthful of food for a variety of clients—from global pharmaceuticals to incorrigible startups. Other people named Sharlene King include a pilates instructor, a British MMA fighter, and a wombat conservationist.

Francisco Inchauste is a designer and writer who tries to create meaningful digital things—which he's found is a lot harder than it sounds. He's an interaction designer, working at Universal Mind, and currently the UX Design editor for Smashing Magazine. He likes to tweet a lot (@iamFinch) and sometimes finds time to blog at GetFinch.com.

✤

Write for DISTANCE

Distance is an attempt to create a good place for both readers *and* writers, and it wouldn't be anything without the contributions of others. **This means you.** We have a track record of publishing well-edited, researched essays that ask the big *why* questions about our field.

Most of *Distance*'s authors have written for us after reading an issue, and so far, every single author of a *Distance* essay has expressed interest in writing more frequently. Writing for us gives people the momentum and confidence to keep at it; towards that end, we love working with people who don't have long track records of successful writing.

If you have a great idea, we can make something fantastic together. Please don't hesitate to email us at we@distance.cc; we'll start small, bat ideas around, and turn it into something great.

✤

Our Sponsors

It doesn't matter how well you designed it if you don't get it built right. Save yourself a lot of frustration and collaborate with developers who understand your way of working. **Hire us at Fingertips.** http://www.fngtps.com

"You look at Longform, which I think is spectacular, and you go 'This is so fucking beautiful.'" — David Carr

Longform for iPad: The best writing on the web, without the web. http://longformapp.com

"The distance is nothing; it is only the first step that is difficult." — Madame Du Deffand

Take the first step toward the journey of your lifetime. Work with me at http://deloittedigital.com/careers.

— Nick Finck

Creating engaging interactive experiences from the heart of Logan Square in Chicago. **Bright Bright Great.** http://brightbrightgreat.com

Dear finicky designers,
Fuck off.

Sincerely,
— **Cards Against Humanity**

Sponsor **DISTANCE**: http://distance.cc/sponsor/

Colophon

Text and subheaders are set in Documenta, made by Frank E. Blokland and distributed through Dutch Type Library. Captions, block quotes, and footnotes are set in Documenta Sans. Headers and paragraph numbers are set in Flama by Mário Feliciano. Fleurons are from Fell Flowers, a free font by Igino Marini.

All errata are at http://distance.cc/errata/. While all cited links were active at the time of publication, if you find a dead URL that's not listed on the errata page, please get in touch.

We support open publication standards and a freer conversation. Visit **The Publication Standards Project** at http://pubstandards.org.

Distance is proudly made in Chicago.

ISBN 978-0-9850515-1-8

Get in touch:
http://distance.cc
we@distance.cc

US $20.00

9 780985 051518 >